Ramayana

A Graded Reader for Teenagers

Retold by
Seema Gupta

Illustrated by
Prosenjit Saha

V&S PUBLISHERS

Published by:

F-2/16, Ansari Road, Daryaganj, New Delhi-110002
☎ 011-23240026, 011-23240027 • *Fax:* 011-23240028
Email: info@vspublishers.com • *Website:* www.vspublishers.com

Branch : Hyderabad
5-1-707/1, Brij Bhawan (Beside Central Bank of India Lane)
Bank Street, Koti, Hyderabad - 500 095
☎ 040-24737290
E-mail: vspublishershyd@gmail.com

Follow us on:

For any assistance sms **VSPUB** to **56161**

All books available at **www.vspublishers.com**

© **Copyright:** *V&S PUBLISHERS*
ISBN 978-93-815885-6-7
Edition 2012

Printed at : Param Offseters, Okhla, New Delhi-110020

Publisherës Note

The original *Ramayana* was a 24,000 couplet-long epic poem attributed to the Sanskrit poet Valmiki. Oral versions of the *Ramayana* circulated for centuries, and the epic was probably first written down sometime around the start of the Common Era. It has since been told, retold, translated and transcreated throughout South and Southeast Asia, and the *Ramayana* continues to be performed in dance, drama, puppet shows, songs and movies all across Asia and the world alike.

The *Ramayana* furnishes the ideals and wisdom of common life. From childhood most Indians learn the characters – Rama, Sita, Lakshmana, Hanuman, Ravana, Dasaratha and others – and incidents of this great epic. The epic helps to bind together people of India, transcending caste, distance and language.

Throughout the centuries, countless versions of the *Ramayana* have been produced in numerous formats and languages for readers of all ages. But previous English versions have been either too short to capture the magnitude of the original or too bulky to finish in one sitting. In this special version of *Ramayana*, author Seema Gupta has rendered the tale in lyrical prose that conveys all the beauty and excitement of the original, while making this spiritual and literary classic accessible to a new generation of readers, specially for the teenagers. With amazing and captivating illustrations this masterpiece surely will satisfy your intellectual and visual thirst for knowledge.

Dedication

Dedicated to my twin sons Amit and Arpit
for being the light of my life

Contents

Sundar Kand

Yuddha Kand

Uttara Kand

Introduction to Ramayana

The Ramayana was originally written by Sage Valmiki in Sanskrit. The original Ramayana is said to have been composed based on each of the twenty-four letters of the Gayatri Hymn. Later Ramayana was translated into the Awadhi language by Goswami Tulsidas as 'Ramcharitmanas'. It contains couplets in verse form called chaupai. The Ramayana has been traditionally divided into seven books, dealing with the life of Rama starting from his birth till his death.

1. ***Bal Kand*** – This is the book about young prince Rama which details the miraculous birth of Rama, his early life in Ayodhya, and his slaying of the demons at the Dandaka forest on the request of Vishwamitra. The book concludes with his wedding to Sita. Bal Kand has 77 chapters.

2. ***Ayodhya Kand*** – This is the book about Ayodhya in which Dasharatha comes to grief over his pledge to Kaikeyi and is forced to send Rama to exile. The book concludes with the death of Dasharatha. Ayodhya Kand has 119 chapters.

3. ***Aranya Kand*** – This is the book about forest which describes the life of Rama, Lakshmana, and Sita in the forest. The book concludes with the abduction of Sita by Ravana. This book has 75 chapters.

4. ***Kishkindha Kand*** – This book is about Kishkindha, the Vanara kingdom in which Rama befriends Sugriva and his army and begins the search for Sita. This book has 67 chapters.

5. ***Sundar Kand*** – This is the book of Sundar (Hanuman) in which Hanuman travels to Lanka in search of Sita. On finding Sita imprisoned there he burns the golden Lanka before returning to Rama to give him the good news. Sundar Kand has 68 chapters.

6. ***Yuddha Kand*** – This is the book about the war which narrates the Rama–Ravana war. The book concludes with the return of successful Rama to Ayodhya and his coronation. This book is the largest of all and it has 131 chapters.

7. ***Uttara Kand*** – This is the seventh book which details the life of Rama and Sita after their return to Ayodhya, Sita's banishment, and the birth of her twin sons in the hermitage of Valmiki.

Main Characters in Ramayana

➤ **Rama** is the hero of the epic Ramayana. He is portrayed as an incarnation of Lord Vishnu. He is the eldest and the favourite son of Dasharatha, the king of Ayodhya. He is a popular prince loved by one and all. He is the epitome of virtue. Dasharatha, forced by one of his wives Kaikeyi, commands Rama to relinquish his right to the throne for fourteen years and go into exile. Rama obeys his father unquestioningly and while in exile, Rama kills the demon king Ravana.

➤ **Sita** is the beloved wife of Rama and the daughter of Janaka, the king of Mithila. She is the incarnation of Goddess Lakshmi (Lord Vishnu's wife). Sita is the epitome of womanly purity and virtue. She follows her husband into exile and there she is abducted by Ravana, the king of Lanka. Rama rescues her by defeating the demon king Ravana.

➤ **Hanuman** is a *vanara* (monkey) belonging to the kingdom of Kishkindha. He worships Rama and helps him find Sita by going to Lanka after crossing the great ocean in one giant leap.

➤ **Lakshmana**, the younger brother of Rama, chooses to go into exile with Rama. He spends his time in exile protecting Sita and Rama. He is deceived by Ravana and Mareecha into believing that Rama was in trouble. This leads to the abduction of Sita.

➤ **Ravana**, a *rakshasa* (demon), is the king of Lanka. He was also the most intelligent and erudite living being of his time. He has ten heads and twenty arms. He received a boon from Lord Brahma that he will not be killed by either gods, demons, or by spirits. After receiving this boon from Brahma, Ravana begins to act wicked and disturbs the deeds of good Brahmins. Rama, a human, is born to defeat him, thus overcoming the boon given by Brahma.

➤ **Dasharatha** is the king of Ayodhya and father of Rama. He has three queens – Kaushalya, Sumitra, and Kaikeyi. Besides Rama he has three other sons – Bharata, Lakshmana, and Shatrughana. Kaikeyi, Dasharatha's favourite queen, forces him to make her son Bharata heir apparent and send Rama into exile. Dasharatha dies heartbroken after Rama goes into exile.

- ➤ **Bharata** is the son of Dasharatha from Kaikeyi. When he learns that his mother Kaikeyi had forced Rama into exile and caused Dasharatha to die broken hearted, he storms out of the palace and goes in search of Rama. When Rama refuses to break his exile and return to the capital to assume the throne, he gets Rama's *khadauns* (sandals) and places them on the throne. Bharata then rules Ayodhya representing Rama for the duration of his exile.

- ➤ **Shatrughana** is the twin son of Dasharatha from Sumitra. Lakshmana is his other twin.

- ➤ **Vishwamitra** is the sage who takes Rama into the forest at the behest of defeating the demons destroying his Vedic sacrifices. On the way back he takes Rama into Mithila where Rama breaks Shiva's bow in Sita's swayamvar and marries Sita.

There are many other characters that play important roles in the great epic – Ramayana. We shall meet them as we proceed in this timeless saga through each kand.

Bal Kand

# Youthful Majesties

Brahma, the creator of this universe, could not revoke a boon he gave to the demon king Ravana, as a reward for his severe penance. The boon was that Ravana could not be slain by gods, demons, or spirits. Having been thus rewarded, Ravana, with the help of his evil supporters, the Rakshasas, began to trouble the Brahmin priests, disturbing their sacrifices. All the gods, watching this devastation, went to Brahma to find a way to end this evil. Brahma went to Vishnu and conveyed the anguish of the gods and requested that Vishnu incarnate on the earth as a human to destroy Ravana, as Ravana had not asked for protection against humans or beasts while seeking the boon from Brahma.

Meanwhile, the good king Dasharatha of Ayodhya, who had ruled over the kingdom of Kosala for a long time, was getting anxious about his successor, for he had no sons to take over the kingdom after him. Taking advice from his ministers and priests, Dasharatha organised a *Putra Prapti Yagya*, a sacrifice for the progeny. Vishnu agreed to be born as the eldest son to Dasharatha and save the world from the atrocities of Ravana.

Birth of Rama

*I*t was a cold morning. The *breeze*[1] felt refreshing on his face. The sky was clear and the sun was about to begin its journey for the day.

There was freshness everywhere and everyone looked cheerful as Ayodhya, the capital of the kingdom of Kosala, woke up to another day.

Dasharatha left his royal bed and looked out of the palace window. Suddenly his eyes fell on a man going to the fields holding his small son's hand. Dasharatha's eyes *moistened*[2]. This was one feeling he could never experience. He had everything in life except for an *heir*[3]. How he wished he could also play with his own child. Alas! Was he destined to be the last king of Surya Vansha.

This dynasty began with the legendary king Manu. Manu was the son of *Surya*, the Sun God and the first ruler of mankind.

Ikshvaku was Manu's eldest son. After Manu, *Surya Vansha* saw famous and glorious kings like Satyavadi Harishchandra, Sagar, Asmanjas, Anshuman, Bhagiratha, Dileep, Raghu, Aja, and Dasharatha.

King Dasharatha was a just and responsible ruler. He ruled his empire with the help of eight highly qualified ministers. Sumantra was the chief among these ministers. Besides the ministers, royal priests Vashishtha, Vamdeva, and Jabali guided him in all spiritual matters.

But one thing *eluded*[4] Dasharatha. He *yearned*[5] for a child. Dasharatha had three beautiful queens – Kaushalya, Sumitra, and Kaikeyi. But none was able to bear him a child.

With a sigh, Dasharatha turned back and got on with his daily routine. By the time he reached the royal court, it was almost noon. Seeing their king distraught, all the ministers asked Sumantra, the Chief Minister to ask the king if he was not feeling well.

With a heavy heart, King Dasharatha disclosed his *plight*[6] to his ministers and the priests.

---

1. *breeze – gentle wind*
2. *moistened – wet*
3. *heir – successor*

4. *eluded – escaped*
5. *yearned – to crave for*
6. *plight – dilemma*

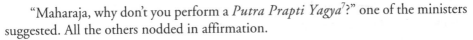

"Maharaja, why don't you perform a *Putra Prapti Yagya*[7]?" one of the ministers suggested. All the others nodded in affirmation.

Sumantra immediately proposed that the great Sage Rishyasringa should be invited to perform this *Yagya*[8]. Dasharatha *consented*[9] and soon a messenger was on the way to Sage Rishyasringa.

Sage Rishyasringa began the *Yagya* at the auspicious moment by lighting the holy fire. The entire place resounded with the holy chanting of sacred Vedic hymns. The smoke from the sacred fire, fragrant with sandalwood and incense, rose high up into the sky.

As the *Yagya* was going on in Ayodhya, the gods in heaven gathered together for an important discussion. The gods told Brahma, the creator of the universe, 'The demon king Ravana is creating havoc all over the three worlds. Many years ago, you gave Ravana a boon as a reward for his thousand-year *penance*[10]. He wanted to be *invincible*[11] so that

7. *Putra Prapti Yagya – yagya performed to get a son*   10. *penance – atonement*
8. *Yagya – holy ritual*   11. *invincible – unbeatable*
9. *consented – agreed*

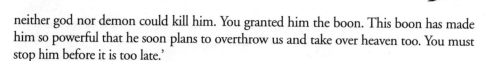

neither god nor demon could kill him. You granted him the boon. This boon has made him so powerful that he soon plans to overthrow us and take over heaven too. You must stop him before it is too late.'

'Yes, I must do something to save this world.' thought Brahma. As he looked down and saw the flames of King Dasharatha's *Yagya* grow higher up in the sky, an idea struck him, 'I shall ask Vishnu, the preserver of the universe to be born on earth in King Dasharatha's house as his son,' *contemplated*[12] Brahma.

Vishnu, when asked, agreed to be born on earth as Dasharatha's son in order to defeat the demon king Ravana. As soon as the gods had made this plan, the *Yagya*-fire began to glow with a golden light.

Everyone looked up in amazement as the tall golden divine figure of *Agni Deva*[13] appeared in the flames. His skin glowed and his hair was tinged with a golden shade like a lion's mane. He was holding a golden bowl in his hands. The bowl was filled with *kheer*[14]. He looked King Dasharatha in his eye and announced, "The Gods are pleased with your *Yagya*. They have sent this gift for you." He handed over the golden bowl to the king and said in a sweet voice, "This is *kheer prasadam*. Give this *sacred*[15] *kheer* to your three wives and you will be blessed with children."

Sage Rishyasringa motioned Dasharatha to go to his palace and give the *kheer* to the three queens as directed by Agni Deva. King Dasharatha first went to Queen Kaushalya's chamber and gave her half of the bowl of *kheer*. He gave one half of what remained to his second queen Sumitra. The third queen, Kaikeyi, got the half of what was left in the bowl. Dasharatha gave the remainder of the *kheer* in the bowl to Sumitra with Kaushalya and Kaikeyi's permission.

Soon Lord Vishnu found his way into the womb of Queen Kaushalya. Time rolled by happily till the moment arrived for the Lord to take birth in human form. The entire world danced in *sheer*[16] delight as Lord Rama, came down to earth. It was the ninth day (*Navami*) of the bright half (*Shukla Paksha*) of the sacred month of *Chaitra*.

The queens gave birth to four sons. Lord Rama was born to Queen Kaushalya. Queen Kaikeyi gave birth to Bharata and Queen Sumitra, who ate the *kheer* twice, gave birth to twin sons Lakshmana and Shatrughana.

King Dasharatha celebrated the occasion with much fanfare. A *gala*[17] ceremony was held in the palace. The entire city of Ayodhya wore festive look. There was no end to the joy among the king and his subjects.

12. *contemplated – thought*
13. *agni deva – God of fire*
14. *kheer – rice pudding*

15. *sacred – holy*
16. *sheer - pure*
17. *gala – huge*

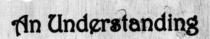

An Understanding

Q & A

Q. Who was the king of Ayodhya?

Ans. _____

_____

Q. Who was Sumantra?

Ans. _____

_____

Q. Who performed the *Putra Prapti Yagya* for the king?

Ans. _____

_____

Q. Who brought Kheer for the king?

Ans. _____

_____

Q. Who was born as Rama in Dasharatha's palace?

Ans. _____

_____

Fill in the blanks

1. ………..... was the eldest son of Manu.

2. Ayodhya was the capital of the kingdom of...............

3. King Dasharatha had .... queens.

4. .... is the creator of the universe.

5. Sumitra gave birth to .... sons.

Match the following

Column I	Column II
Kaushalya	Lakshmana and a Shatrughana
Sumitra	Bharata
Kaikeyi	Rama

Life-sketch

Prepare a life-sketch of King Dasharatha describing his strengths and weaknesses.

_____

_____

Food for Thought

If King Dasharatha had given the entire bowl of kheer to Kaushalya, how would that have altered the Ramayana?

Write a diary entry as Dasharatha when he hears the news of the birth of his sons.

Life Skills

Yagyas are a part of our culture and tradition which go a long way back to Vedic times. The manner, in which *Yagya* is performed today, may have slightly changed but the essence of this Vedic ritual still remains the same. Find out more about *Yagya* and its importance in Hinduism.

Vishwamitra's Arrival

The four young princes were very handsome. Though the four of them were very caring and *affectionate*[1] towards each other, Lakshmana stayed mostly with Rama while Bharata and Shatrughana stayed together. Whenever the four princes walked through the lanes of Ayodhya everyone watched them.

When the four princes grew up, it was time to send them to the *gurukul*[2] of Sage Vashishtha to attain knowledge of the Vedas and other texts. Before sending the princes to *gurukul* for higher studies, *Yagyopavita*[3] ceremony of all the four princes was held. They were invested with a sacred thread before being sent to the hermitage of Sage Vashishtha for their formal education.

All the four brother were endowed with wisdom and virtues. In a very short time, they learnt the Vedas, Puranas, and all the other Shastras.

The brothers grew up to be fine gentlemen with *virtues*[4] of *humility*[5] and respect towards elders. Everyone's heart soared with happiness and filled with pride at the sight of such glorious princes.

Soon it was time for the princes to return home. A joyous king Dasharatha sent Sumantra to Sage Vashishtha's hermitage to bring the four princes back to Ayodhya.

The *chariot*[6] carrying the four princes, clad in the royal robes, reached the gates of the palace. Citizens of Ayodhya were *overwhelmed*[7] with joy to see Rama, Lakshmana, Bharata, and Shatrughana. Everyone rejoiced in the city of Ayodhya.

One day a messenger came to King Dasharatha to announce the arrival of the great Sage Vishwamitra.

Everyone rushed in to make the sage comfortable as everyone feared him. Sage Vishwamitra, though famed for his wisdom and divine *perception*[8], had a very bad temper.

King Dasharatha touched Sage Vishwamitra's feet. Then he folded his palms and

---

1. *affectionate – loving*
2. *gurukul – boarding school*
3. *Yagyopavita – holy thread*
4. *virtue – quality*

5. *humility – modesty*
6. *chariot – vehicle*
7. *overwhelmed – besieged*
8. *perception – insight*

said to him, "I am truly blessed by your presence, O sage. What brings you here? Please tell me what can I do for you?"

He hovered around the sage anxiously, urging him to eat a little fruit or drink some milk. Touched by Dasharatha's *hospitality*[9], Vishwamitra felt happy.

After he had eaten and rested, Vishwamitra explained the reason for his visit. "King, I am performing a *Yagya*. Two powerful demons have been trying to obstruct my *Yagya*. These demons are Mareecha and Subahu. They have been troubling me during prayers and *Yagya* by showering blood and bones on the sacred fire. I want you to send your brave sons Rama and Lakshmana with me to kill all these powerful demons."

Dasharatha was stunned. He *shuddered*[10] to think of sending his beloved sons to those *dreadful*[11] demons. Vishwamitra's request left him speechless.

It was at this moment that Sage Vashishtha *intervened*[12] and said softly, "Dear King, let Rama and Lakshmana go with Vishwamitra. The whole world knows that Vishwamitra

9. *hospitality – welcome*
10. *shuddered – trembled*

11. *dreadful – terrible*
12. *intervened – interfere*

is the bravest of the brave. He is the master of every weapon on the earth as well as in heaven. Do you think he cannot defeat the demons himself?

Oh yes, he can do that by merely lifting his finger. Yet he wants your sons to accompany him to perform this *task*[13]. He asks them because he wants to do them good. So don't worry. Send the princes with him to the forest. O king, do not fear for their safety. They are in good hands."

Sage Vashishtha's words reassured Dasharatha. He bowed before the wishes of the sage and called upon Rama and Lakshmana to go to the forest with sage Vishwamitra.

Next day, at the crack of dawn, Rama and Lakshmana set out with sage Vishwamitra. The journey was difficult. The path was uneven and filled with thorns. Soon they reached Sarayu River.

After they crossed the river, the banks suddenly became narrow and they found themselves standing before a *dense*[14] forest.

---

13. *task – job*   14. *dense – thick*

An Understanding

Q & A

Q. Where did the four princes complete their education?

Ans. _____

_____

Q. Name the ceremony held for the four princes before they were sent to gurukul?

Ans. _____

_____

Q. Who was Sage Vishwamitra?

Ans. _____

_____

Q. Why did he want Rama and Lakshmana to accompany him?

Ans. _____

_____

Q. Which river did Rama and Lakshmana cross along with Sage Vishwamitra?

Ans. _____

_____

Yes or No

1. The four princes were very handsome. _____

2. King Dasharatha ignored Sage Vishwamitra when he came to meet him.

_____

3. Sage Vishwamitra taught the princes about Vedas and other texts.

_____

4. King Dasharatha did not want Rama and Lakshmana to go with Sage Vishwamitra. _____

5. Rama and Lakshmana refused to accompany Sage Vishwamitra.

_____

Make Sentence

Write meanings of these phrases and make sentences with them

1. Flare up: _____

   _____

2. Give up: _____

   _____

3. Set up: _____

   _____

4. Stuck up: _____

   _____

5. Sum up: _____

Food for Thought

What would have happened if King Dasharatha sent Bharata and Shatrughana instead of Rama and Lakshmana to the forest with Sage Vishwamitra?

Life Skills

Yagyopavita ceremony is still being performed in some castes in our country. Have you ever seen such a ceremony being performed? Find out more about this ritual. Discuss its significance and importance in modern times. Write a short note based on your findings.

3

Tadaka, Mareecha, and Subahu

"This is the forest of Dandaka." said Vishwamitra. "Once upon a time, this forest was a beautiful place where men, birds, animals, and insects lived together happily. Then one day, Tadaka, a terrible demoness came to live here and this place trembled under her *evil*[1] deeds. She is out here to destroy all of us. When any sage performs a *Yagya* in his hermitage in this forest, she comes and kills everyone around. She throws

1. *evil – wicked*

dead animals and showers bones in the sacred fire. No one can beat her, she is as strong as a thousand elephants."

Pointing towards a small hill close by, Vishwamitra paused and said, "Look, there is her cave. She lives here. She can smell humans from afar. I want you to draw her out of her cave and kill her. She is evil and this is the right *fate²* for her."

Without a moment's hesitation, Rama and Lakshmana went towards the cave. Rama put his hand on his bow. The twanging of its string made the entire forest *reverberate³*.

Tadaka, who was taking a nap in her cave got up, "What was that sound?" She opened her eyes in surprise, "That sounded like a bow! Who dares to enter my forest?" She leapt out of the cave.

Like all demons, Tadaka knew magic. She caused a rain of pebbles and stones on Rama and Lakshmana. But the two brothers did not move and the stones rattled down, far away from them.

---

2. *fate – destiny*   3. *reverberate – echo*

This angered Tadaka and she rushed towards them *furiously*[4]. The entire ground moved under her heavy footsteps. But Rama was ready for her. She was a little distance away from them when Rama shot a single arrow at her. The arrow went straight into her heart. Tadaka fell down with a *scream*[5].

The moment Tadaka died, the gloom and *sinister*[6] feel of the forest disappeared. Sunshine filled the entire place. Trees began to flower and fruits appeared on them. Birds started chirping and animals moved around freely.

"Rama, bless you, my son. You have given a new life to this forest. You are truly born to save the world from malice and *impiety*[7]. I shall bless you with several mighty weapons which will help you later in life." Saying so Vishwamitra offered Rama the powerful weapons – *Dandachakra, Kaalchakra, Brahmastra,* and others.

Vishwamitra taught them all the rare *mantras* for getting divine weapons which he had learnt from Lord Shiva after years of worship and penance. He taught them how to *summon*[8] each weapon and how to send them in the right direction and then how to bring them back.

Rama and Lakshmana continued their journey with Sage Vishwamitra. Finally they reached Siddhashram, which was his hermitage. After they settled down, Vishwamitra proceeded to begin the *Yagya*. For five days, the *Yagya* continued *uninterrupted*[9]. On the sixth day, there was a loud rumbling noise like that of thundering clouds coming from the sky. Two giant demons appeared from nowhere. One of them was Mareecha, the son of Tadaka who was killed by Rama in Dandaka forest. The other demon was his friend Subahu.

Rama looked up. Mareecha and Subahu stood there with their hair steamed out and knotted. Their eyes were as red as blood and glowed like shining coal with the *meanness*[10] in their heart. Following them was a huge army of demons.

Screaming with terror, all the sages ran inside the hermitage, only Vishwamitra waited by the *Yagya*, accompanied by Rama and Lakshmana.

As Mareecha charged towards them, the two princes stood unmoved with their minds working rapidly. They knew that even hundreds of ordinary arrows were not enough to kill a *ferocious*[11] demon such as Mareecha. Rama began to *chant*[12] the *mantra* for divine weapons as taught to him by Sage Vishwamitra. Thunder roared, lightning flashed as *Manavastra* came flying towards Mareecha.

He sank instantly to the bottom of the earth.

---

4. *furiously – angrily*
5. *scream – shout*
6. *sinister – evil*
7. *impiety – wickedness*
8. *summon – call*

9. *Uninterrupted – Nonstop*
10. *Meanness – Unkindness*
11. *Ferocious – Brutal*
12. *Chant – Recite*

Then Rama closed his eyes and beckoned another divine weapon, *Agneyastra*. He hurled it at Subahu. *Agneyastra*, created by *Agni*, the god of fire, began to burn Subahu. Within moments, he was just a heap of ashes on the ground.

All the sages came out of the ashram. They were all very happy now. They thanked Rama and Lakshmana and blessed them for bringing peace once more to their ashram. Sage Vishwamitra embraced Rama and praised him.

An Understanding

Q & A

Q. What was the name of the forest where Tadaka lived?

Ans. _____

_____

Q. How did Sage Vishwamitra want Rama and Lakshmana to kill Tadaka?

Ans. _____

_____

Q. Name three divine weapons that Sage Vishwamitra gave to Rama.

Ans. _____

_____

Q. What was the name of Sage Vishwamitra's hermitage?

Ans. _____

_____

Q. Which of the remaining two demons was killed by Rama?

Ans. _____

_____

True & False

Write T for true and F for false statements. Rewrite the false ones with the correct information

1. Tadaka lived in a magnificent palace.

_____

_____

2. Unlike all demons, Tadaka knew magic.

_____

_____

3. Rama killed Tadaka with a single arrow.

_____

_____

4. Sage Vishwamitra performed *Yagya* uninterrupted for five days.

    _____

    _____

5. Rama used Manavastra to kill Subahu.

    _____

    _____

Fill in the blanks

Complete this paragraph by filling in the ten missing words

After they settled down, ... proceeded to begin the .... For five days, the *Yagya* continued .... On the .... day, there was a loud rumbling noise like that of .... clouds coming from the sky. Two giant .... appeared from nowhere. One of them was .... a, the son of .... who was killed by Rama in .... forest. The other demon was his friend ....

Food for Thought

Imagine all the divine weapons of Rama failed to kill Tadaka. In her fury, she took away Rama and Lakshmana to her cave. What would Sage Vishwamitra do now?

Life Skills

We read about powerful weapons of ancient times like *Dandachakra, Kaalchakra, Brahmastra, Manavastra,* and *Agneyastra.* However in modern age also we have many powerful weapons like gun, bullet, missile, etc. Both types of weapons are equally destructive in nature then why do we condemn the modern weapons while praise the ancient ones?

Sage Gautama and Ahalya

he next day, Rama and Lakshmana set out on their journey towards Mithila with Sage Vishwamitra. Along the forest paths, they saw a hermitage surrounded by tall trees laden with fruits.

"Why is this ashram so *desolate*[1]? Does no one live here?"asked Rama.

Vishwamitra told him, "This is the ashram of Sage Gautama. Long ago, he lived

---

1. *desolate – isolated*

here with his beautiful wife Ahalya. One day, as he was away, Indra, the king of gods, *disguised*[2] himself as Gautama and came to the ashram to seduce Ahalya. Ahalya felt *flattered*[3] with her husband *bestowing*[4] so much attention on her. She fell in love with him. Little did she know that it was Indra in disguise of her husband. When Indra left and real Gautama returned, he read Ahalya's mind. He was enraged by her lack of faithfulness. He cursed her, 'You shall turn to stone. This beauty which has made you so *vain*[5] and *wayward*[6] will turn into a cold piece of rock.'

Ahalya turned into a statue of stone the moment sage Gautama said these words.

After the initial shock, Gautama realised that his wife was not at fault. But the damage was already done. He could not take his curse back so he said, 'When Rama, the son of Ayodhya's king Dasharatha, will visit this place, you will regain your original form.'

So here stands the statue of Ahalya. If you touch her she will be able to come back to her real form." Saying so, Vishwamitra pointed towards a beautiful stone figure of a woman.

Moved by *compassion*[7], Rama stepped forward in wonder and reached out to touch the statue. There was a sudden *rustling*[8] sound. The stone figure transformed into a human form. Ahalya emerged out of the stone. Sage Gautama too accepted Ahalya as his wife.

---

2. *disguised – camouflaged*
3. *flattered – thrilled*
4. *bestow – impart*
5. *vain – foolish*

6. *wayward – errant*
7. *compassion – sympathy*
8. *rustle – crackle*

An Understanding

Q & A

Q. Who was Ahalya?

Ans. _____

_____

Q. Who came to her in disguise of Sage Gautama?

Ans. _____

_____

Q. What was the curse of Gautama?

Ans. _____

_____

Q. How could the curse be broken?

Ans. _____

_____

Q. Describe the desolate ashram of Gautama in your own words.

Ans. _____

_____

_____

_____

Life-sketch

Prepare a life-sketch of Sage Gautama and his wife Ahalya describing their nature and character as you grasp from the story.

_____

_____

_____

_____

Food for Thought

Do you think it was right of Sage Gautama to penalise Ahalya for an offense committed by Indra? Who should have been the right person to be punished?

Life Skills

An ashram or a hermitage was a place which was set up in cool confines of nature. The ascetics and sages of yore lived there and indulged in sacred rituals. However the concept of ashram is still prevalent in India and we hear of many ashrams in different parts of our country. How different do you feel are the modern ashrams from the ashrams of ancient times? Write a short paragraph on it.

Sita Swayamvara

Having spent the night at Sage Gautama's ashram, Sage Vishwamitra, along with Rama and Lakshmana, continued the journey towards Mithila, the capital of King Janaka.

Vishwamitra and the two princes were personally welcomed by King Janaka on their arrival to Mithila. Janaka was performing a *Yagya* and was happy to have them over.

Next day everyone gathered at the venue of *Yagya* which was magnificent. After the *Yagya* was over, it was time for Sita's *Swayamvara*[1]. Soon the famous Shiva bow

1. *swayamvara – an old custom of a girl choosing her own husband*

called 'Sunabh' was brought to the venue of swayamvara. Handsome kings and young princes decked up in pearls and diamonds in their finest *attire*[2] from all the neighbouring kingdoms were all seated around the bow which had been kept on a huge eight-wheeled cart .

Rama and Lakshmana walked in with Sage Vishwamitra and sat down in one corner quietly.

The trumpets rang out when King Janaka motioned for the swayamvara to begin. Everyone was quiet as King Janaka addressed them all, "This is the *mighty*[3] bow which was given to one of my ancestors by Lord Shiva himself. Till date no one has been able to lift it let alone string it. Today I have placed it here. The bravest and the mightiest who can string this mighty bow shall wed my daughter Sita."

A *murmur*[4] ran through the hall.

One by one all the princes, noblemen, kings flexed up their muscles, tightened their belts and came up and tried to pick up the bow. But not a single one could even move it from its place. Some even collapsed from the effort and had to be carried out.

King Janaka was shocked beyond words. When the last of the kings failed in the mission, he spoke in *anguish*[5], "I am convinced that there are no heroes left on

2. *attire – dress*	4.	*murmur – whisper*
3. *mighty – powerful*	5.	*anguish – sorrow*

this earth anymore. It seems that *destiny*[6] wills that my daughter Sita should remain unmarried all her life. If I knew the earth was devoid of brave and strong men, I would never have taken such a *vow*[7]."

Rama looked at Vishwamitra who smiled at him and nodded in agreement. The young prince got up and walked towards the bow.

Rama picked up the bow as if it were a feather and strung it swiftly. His movements were so quick that before anyone could realise what was happening, he had already fulfilled the vow taken by King Janaka. At that instant, there was a great clap of thunder and the bow broke into two pieces. The earth shook and the mountains roared. The water in the oceans rose and Surya's chariot began to *swerve*[8] from its daily path across the sky.

The quiet of the *Yagya* place was broken by the sound of drums and horns from heavens above. The gods showered flowers on Rama in his praise. The gods watching from heaven *applauded*[9] while *Gandharvas*, the divine singers, began to sing Rama's praises.

King Janaka came out of his *stupor*[10] and announced formally that this prince of Ayodhya had won his daughter Sita's hand.

After Sita wed Rama by placing a garland around his neck, messengers were sent to King Dasharatha to inform him of the good news. Dasharatha came at once, accompanied by his queens, to attend the wedding. His heart filled with pride when he heard of the *feat*[11] performed by his loving son Rama.

King Janaka's brother Kushadhwaj, who was the king of Sankasya, had two charming daughters Mandavi and Shrutkirti. The two sages, Vashishtha and Vishwamitra jointly proposed that Mandavi and Shrutkirti be married to Bharata and Shatrughana respectively while Lakshmana was chosen to marry Sita's younger sister Urmila.

Thus, at the same altar, the four brothers were married. Rama married Sita, Lakshmana married Urmila, Bharata married Mandavi, and Shatrughana married Shrutkirti.

For ten days, Mithila resembled Indra's celestial city Indrapuri with unending celebrations going on as Rama and Sita were joined in an *eternal*[12] bond.

---

6. *destiny – fate*
7. *vow – pledge*
8. *swerve – change direction*
9. *applauded – highly praised*

10. *stupor – daze*
11. *feat – achievement*
12. *eternal – timeless*

An Understanding

Q & A

Q. Who was the king of Mithila?

Ans. _____

_____

Q. What was the name of the King's daughter whose swayamvara was organised in Mithila?

Ans. _____

_____

Q. What was the condition to win the swayamvara?

Ans. _____

_____

Q. Why was the King shocked?

Ans. _____

_____

Q. Who won Sita's hand in the swayamvara?

Ans. _____

_____

Who & Whom

Write to whom the King would have said these words?

1. 'Welcome sage! It is an honour to have you and the princes here.'……………………………..

2. 'Start the swayamvara.'……………………………

3. 'I shall give my daughter's hand in marriage to the man who strings this mighty bow.' …………..

4. 'If I knew the earth was devoid of brave and strong men…'………………….

5. 'May God bless the couple.'…………………….

Complete the Table

Complete this table by writing how they are related to each other

	Sita	Urmila	Mandavi	Shrutkiriti
1. King Janaka				
2. King Kushadhwaj				
3. Rama				
4. Lakshmana				
5. Bharata				
6. Shatrughana				

Food for Thought

What would have happened if Rama was unable to break Shiva's bow in Swayamvara?

Life Skills

The practice of swayamvara allows a girl to choose her own groom. Does our modern society also allow a girl the freedom to select her husband? Get information about incidents of honour killings that have been taking place in our society and write an article about which society could be called more liberal - the modern one or the ancient one?

Ayodhya Kand

Tumultuous Times

After Rama got married to Sita and entered Grihasthashram, King Dasharatha decided to hand over the reins of his empire to Rama and coronate him as the crown prince. Dasharatha had begun to feel weary with age now. The citizens of Ayodhya received the announcement of his desire with delight and the whole city was ready for the most splendid preparations for the ceremony. Dasharatha went to discuss the celebrations with his wives.

Alas! Fate had something else in store for him. What he had planned for tomorrow could not be, because destiny had willed otherwise. This tomorrow came after fourteen years, when Dasharatha was no more to see his son's coronation.

Although Rama was an incarnation of Lord Vishnu himself, he too had to undergo the common suffering, pain, and trauma of an ordinary mortal but with a difference. While an ordinary man would have broken down under the harsh realities of life, Rama kept smiling even in the worst of situations, never for a moment wavering from his duties as a human being. No wonder he was born in the world to set examples for each role in the life of a man living in the society.

He is, therefore, rightfully called *Maryada Purushottam*, who would never deviate from the path of righteous deeds.

Manthara's Devious Plot

*T*he four princes and their brides were now living happily in the magnificent palace at Ayodhya. King Dasharatha too felt *content*[1] whenever he saw them happy. He often thought that the most beautiful day of his life would be when Rama would become the crown prince.

'Once he becomes *Yuvraj*[2] and learns to rule, I can give up the throne and spend my time in prayer. I am sure he will look after Ayodhya better than any other ruler in our dynasty,' thought King Dasharatha.

---

1. *content – happy*   2. *yuvraj – crown prince*

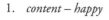

Once the royal decision was taken, there was no reason to hold back the celebrations. The news spread like wildfire. Everyone in the palace was overjoyed at this news.

Kaushalya, Sumitra, and Kaikeyi were very happy. They blessed Rama and wished him luck in his new *endeavour*[3]. Lakshmana was by Rama's side throughout. Bharata and Shatrughana were away at that time, visiting Kaikeyi's father.

Sage Vashishtha fixed the coronation on an *auspicious*[4] day which was not very far.

As everyone in Ayodhya *rejoiced*[5] and made arrangements for Rama's coronation, an old woman watched everything quietly from the window of Kaikeyi's palace. Manthara, a hunchback, was Queen Kaikeyi's maid of many years. Her thoughts were as ugly as her posture and looks.

"O foolish queen, do you know your sun is setting just like this sun setting outside your window. Dasharatha has decided to make Rama the ruler of this land. Now Kaushalya will rise to the fame because Rama is her son." Unable to contain herself any longer, Manthara entered Kaikeyi's chamber and called out to her.

---

3. *endeavour – venture*
4. *auspicious - lucky*

5. *rejoiced – delighted*

Kaikeyi turned to Manthara and said, "I know Manthara. But don't forget Rama is my son too. Today is a day for celebration. Here, take this pearl necklace. I am so happy today." Kaikeyi threw the string of pearls towards Manthara that she was wearing around her neck.

But Manthara threw the necklace to the ground and said, "You are a fool. From tomorrow your son Bharata will be a slave of Rama. Rama will get him killed. You will be reduced to the status of a maid servant."

"What are you talking about?" the gentle queen stopped everything she was doing and sat down to listen *intently*[6] to what Manthara was saying.

Manthara felt *exhilarated*[7] on getting full attention from Kaikeyi. She spoke with *vehemence*[8], "O queen, I always knew you were *naïve*[9] as a dove. Can't you see the danger that lies ahead of you and Bharata when Rama becomes the *yuvraj*? Just think...just give it a thought... why else would King Dasharatha announce Rama's coronation at a time when Bharata is not even in Ayodhya. He knew Bharata would put up a fight for his right. Even you were not consulted before the royal decision was taken. He consulted Kaushalya and took the decision. You were only informed after everything was settled. Do you still need more proof of your declining status in the palace?"

"What shall I do, Manthara? I am scared." Manthara's words were enough to poison the ears of Kaikeyi. She was now worried about the fate of her son Bharata.

Manthara spoke in a soft voice so that no one could overhear them, "Remember, long ago when King Dasharatha was wounded in the battle and fell unconscious, you were the one who drove his chariot out of the battlefield. You took out the arrows from his body and saved his life. Remember, when he became stronger he granted you two wishes. And, recall my dear Kaikeyi, what had you said – I do not need anything now. I will ask later. The time has come now to ask for those wishes. Tell him that your first wish is that he should make Bharata heir to the throne and the second one is that he should *banish*[10] Rama and send him for fourteen years of exile."

Manthara's eyes gleamed with *malice*[11] and *triumph*[12] as she spoke these words. "Go now and lie down in *Kop Bhawan*. Throw all your jewels on the floor. Do not *compromise*[13] on any terms else you know your fate will be that of Kaushalya's slave...."

6. *intently – attentively*
7. *exhilarated – overjoyed*
8. *vehemence – intensity*
9. *naïve – immature*

10. *banish – expel*
11. *malice – hatred*
12. *triumph – victory*
13. *compromise – negotiate*

An Understanding

Q & A

Q. What did King Dasharatha think would be the most beautiful day of his life?

Ans. _____

_____

Q. Who was Manthara?

Ans. _____

_____

Q. Why did Kaikeyi give Manthara a pearl necklace?

Ans. _____

_____

Q. Who had given two boons to Kaikeyi and why?

Ans. _____

_____

Q. Why did Manthara ask Kaikeyi to go to *Kop Bhawan*?

Ans. _____

_____

Complete these sentences

1. The four princes and their brides were now living ....

....

2. Sage Vashishstha fixed the coronation.....................................

....

3. As everyone in Ayodhya rejoiced and made arrangements for Rama's coronation..

4. Kaikeyi threw a string of pearls ....

....

5. Manthara's eyes gleamed with..

....

Who, whom & why

Who said these, to whom, and why?

1. 'Go now and lie down in Kop Bhawan.' ………………………………

2. 'What shall I do, Manthara? I am scared.'……………….................

3. 'I am sure he will look after Ayodhya better than any other ruler in our dynasty.' ………………………………

4. 'O foolish queen, do you know your sun is setting…'.....................
   ………………………………

5. 'Here, take this pearl necklace. I am so happy today.'.....................
   …………………………………..

Food for Thought

Although it was Kaikeyi's decision to ask for those two boons from King Dasharatha, yet Manthara got all the blame for instigating this idea in Kaikeyi's mind. Write a diary entry on Manthara who was detested by everyone later for this evil deed.

Life Skills

Entering the *Kop Bhawan* was a concept highlighted very well in the *Ramayana*. In modern times, we do not have *Kop Bhawans* where we can go and release our anger but the kop (anger) does exist in our life. how do you release your anger? Find out from your parents, neighbours, friends as to how they release their anger. Make a comparative chart and find out the various means of showing your anger.

Rama's Banishment

King Dasharatha went to Queen Kaikeyi's chamber after he received her message to come and meet her immediately.

Not finding her there, he asked her whereabouts from the maids. When he came to know that she was in *Kop Bhawan*, he became panicky and rushed there.

He found Kaikeyi lying on the floor, dressed in an old *saree*. Her hair was *disheveled*[1] and all her jewels were strewn on the floor. She was a picture of someone in *mourning*[2].

Dasharatha *kneeled*[3] beside her and spoke to her softly, "What's wrong, my dear queen. Are you not well? Have you received any bad news? Please tell me. My heart breaks to see you in such a state. Please speak; you know I will do anything for you."

These were the magic words, Kaikeyi was waiting to hear. She immediately opened her eyes and sat up, "I only ask you to grant me those two boons which you had promised me long ago when I saved your life on the battlefield."

The king smiled as he recalled the incident clearly. He nodded in agreement.

Kaikeyi felt assured by his nod and continued further, "The first boon I want is that you make my son Bharata, the *yuvraj* of Ayodhya. The second boon I ask is that you banish Rama to the forest for fourteen years."

Dasharatha recoiled in horror of the boons just now asked by his most beloved queen. His face turned ashen. He felt breath going out of his body and he fell unconscious.

When King Dasharatha regained consciousness, he tried to make Kaikeyi understand the *repercussions*[4] of her wishes. But Kaikeyi was blinded by the dark emotions of jealousy, greed, and *treachery*[5].

She remained unmoved by Dasharatha's tears and pitiful state. The only words she spoke were, "You promised me two boons and now I want them. How can you go back on your word now?"

---

1. *disheveled - unkempt*
2. *mourning – grief*
3. *kneeled - go down on your knees kneeled - go down on your knees*

4. *repercussions – consequences*
5. *treachery – deceit*

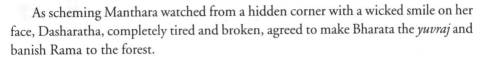

As scheming Manthara watched from a hidden corner with a wicked smile on her face, Dasharatha, completely tired and broken, agreed to make Bharata the *yuvraj* and banish Rama to the forest.

Kaikeyi sent for Rama immediately. When Rama arrived, Kaikeyi told him about the king's decision.

Instead of looking shocked, Rama looked as content as before, "Mother! I know you would never think badly for me. Your word is my command. I shall definitely go to the forest for fourteen years. Bharata is my brother. I am sure he will be a great ruler. My best wishes are always with him. Kindly take care of my father and tell him not to worry for me."

Soon there was a *commotion*[6]. Everyone in Ayodhya had woken up with happiness in their heart as the day for Rama's coronation had dawned. But within a few hours, the entire scenario changed.

6. *commotion – uproar*

Rama went to his mother's chamber to bid her goodbye. Sita was waiting with Kaushalya for him.

Kaushalya had heard the news before Rama could reach her chamber. Tears poured out of her eyes. She quietly pulled her dear son to her heart and let the sorrow in her heart flow.

"I, too, will come with you, my lord." Sita's voice from the far corner broke their *reverie*[7]. Though Rama did not want her to come with him, yet he did not have the heart to refuse her.

Just as they were about to leave, Lakshmana came rushing to them and insisted on accompanying them.

The next day, Rama, Lakshmana, and Sita came out of their palace dressed as hermits and left for the forest in a chariot with Sumantra as their *charioteer*[8].

7. *reverie – daydream*   8. *charioteer – the one who drives a chariot*

An Understanding

Q & A

Q. Where did King Dasharatha find Queen Kaikeyi when he came to see her?

Ans. _____

_____

Q. What were the two boons that Kaikeyi asked from the king?

Ans. _____

_____

Q. How did the king react to those boons?

Ans. _____

_____

Q. Who told Rama about the king's decision?

Ans. _____

_____

Q. Did Rama go alone to the forest? If not then who accompanied him?

Ans. _____

_____

Choose the characters who suit the following words:

1. Wily
2. Devious
3. Innocent
4. Clever
5. Scheming
6. Immature
7. Naïve
8. Foolish

Fill in the blanks

Read these dialogues and fill in the names of the characters who would have spoken them

1. .... went to his mother's chamber to bid her goodbye. He

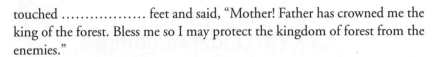
touched .... feet and said, "Mother! Father has crowned me the king of the forest. Bless me so I may protect the kingdom of forest from the enemies."

2. "No, ..., you must not come with me." .... was shocked, "You have been brought up in palaces. You will not be able to live the hard life of forest. You should stay here with mother and father till I complete my exile and come back to you."

3. ....gentle face was flushed with determination as she said to............ "Please do not leave me behind. I will die without you."

4. .... came rushing to .... and .... as they got ready to take leave of .... and said, "I've just heard. You are not going alone. I'm coming with you."

Food for Thought

Do you think it was a wise decision on King Dasharatha's part to banish Rama for fourteen years?

If Rama had not taken Sita and Lakshmana with him, the story of Ramayana would have been different. Frame a short storyline considering Rama went for exile alone.

Life Skills

Discipline is important in life. Parents punish their children or stop them from doing many things which they think are not good for their children. But punishing and banishing are two different things altogether. Write about the difference between these two things citing some examples.

Dasharatha Remembers Shravan Kumar

While Rama, Sita, and Lakshmana moved towards Chitrakoot with Sage Bhardwaj, Sumantra returned to Ayodhya. He went straight to the king's palace. Dasharatha barely seemed alive. He asked Sumantra, "Where is my Rama? Where have you left him? I am not worthy to be his father. Either you take me to him or kill me. I cannot bear this pain."

As the days passed, Dasharatha's condition grew from bad to worse. One day as he sat quietly with Kaushalya, suddenly he remembered a long forgotten curse

inflicted upon him by a blind couple. He clearly remembered the grief he had caused them.

He unburdened his heart to Kaushalya, "Kaushalya, no one can escape the laws of *karma*[1]. We all have to bear the fruits of our actions. Today as I sit here crying for my son I recall a sin which I committed in my youthful days. The time has now come for me to repay for that sin."

It was a lovely day. I had gone hunting in the forest near the bank of river Sarayu. It was getting dark. Suddenly I heard a sound coming from the direction of the stream. I could not see properly as the sun had already set, but the voice clearly indicated as a wild animal was drinking water by the stream. I shot the arrow in the direction of the sound. Then suddenly there was a loud cry of a human being. I was horrified. I rushed to the stream where I saw a horrible sight. It was not a wild animal that my arrow had hit. It had *pierced*[2] the *bosom*[3] of a young boy who lay in a pool of blood."

"Who was he?" asked Kaushalya.

"He was Sharavan Kumar who had taken his blind parents for a pilgrimage carrying them on his shoulders in two baskets strung on either end of a long pole.

As soon as I went near him, he gasped, 'Please sir, take this water to my blind parents. And please do not tell them anything till they have quenched their thirst.' He pointed towards a grove. In the next instant, he fell back as his soul left his body.

I picked up the pot of water. I reached the grove that he had pointed. There I saw a blind old couple. As they heard my footsteps, the old man, who was a learned sage, said, 'Have you brought water, son? Give it to us. We are very thirsty.'

Fearing they might recognise me I did not *utter*[4] a word, but the wise man had sensed that something was wrong. He refused to drink water till I told him the whole story. I had no choice but to tell them all that had happened. The old couple cried until they had no more tears left. Finally the old man spoke, 'O King, you may be a great warrior but you have taken away our soul. We cannot touch a drop of water you have brought for us. We have no reason to live now. We will die – my wife and I – because we cannot live without our dear son, Shravan Kumar. But before I die, I curse you.'

The old man's voice changed and the anger replaced the deep anguish in his voice, 'I curse you, O King Dasharatha, that you too will die grieving for your son.' With these words, the old man and his wife died then and there."

By now, King Dasharatha was barely aware of his surroundings. He simply went

---

1. *karma – duty*
2. *pierced – punctured*
3. *bosom – chest*
4. *utter - speak*

on speaking and staring blankly, "The curse of Shravan's parents has come true today. I can see the blind parents of Shravan Kumar *beckoning*[5] me to join them. My last moment has arrived. I cannot see a thing. O Rama, I have gone blind like Shravan's parents. Where are you? Please come and save me. No one but my Rama can save me from Yama's men. They are coming to get me. Oh, Rama…Ra…ama.." Uttering Rama's name, the king breathed his last.

5. *beckoning – summoning*

An Understanding

Q & A

Q. Why did King Dasharatha go to the bank of the river Sarayu?

Ans. _____

_____

Q. Who was Shravan Kumar?

Ans. _____

_____

Q. Why and where were Shravan's parents waiting for him?

Ans. _____

_____

Q. Why did Shravan's parents not drink water brought by King Dasharatha?

Ans. _____

_____

Q. What did Shravan's father say to Dasharatha?

Ans. _____

_____

Common Error & Correction

These words have the same spelling and pronunciation but different meanings. Write their meanings and make sentences with them

1. bank ....
   bank ....
2. dear ....
   dear ....
3. stream ....
   stream ....
4. tear ....
   tear ....
5. bear ....
   bear ....

Number these events in correct order

1.   The old couple cried until they had no more tears left.

2.   King Dasharatha shot an arrow in the direction of the sound.

3.   The old man and his wife died without drinking a single drop of water.

4.   The old father cursed King Dasharatha.

5.   King Dasharatha took water to the grove.

6.   Shravan Kumar came to the stream to fetch some water.

7.   King Dasharatha went hunting in the forest near the bank of river Sarayu.

8.   While sitting in his palace, King Dasharatha remembered a long forgotten curse inflicted upon him by a blind couple.

9.   The wise old man sensed that something was wrong.

10. Shravan Kumar requested the king to take water to his thirsty parents.

Food for Thought

Write the feelings of Shravan Kumar when he got shot
by King Dasharatha.

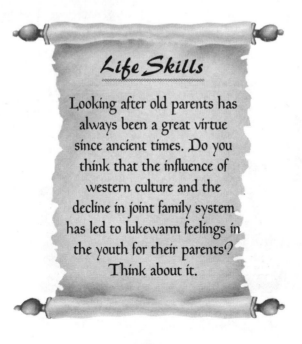

Life Skills

Looking after old parents has always been a great virtue since ancient times. Do you think that the influence of western culture and the decline in joint family system has led to lukewarm feelings in the youth for their parents? Think about it.

Bharata Meets Rama

Bharata and Shatrughana were called from their maternal grandfather's house to perform the last rites of their father. Bharata was angry beyond words when he came to know of the *devious*[1] plot hatched by his mother Kaikeyi. He refused to be a part of it and declared to everyone, "I'll never accept this crown. It belongs to my brother Rama and you all know this fact for sure. It was the king's wish, it's your wish, and this is my wish too. If it had been not for my mother's scheming plot, today Rama would

---

1. *devious – deceitful*

emotions, Rama asked Hanuman in a low voice full of sadness and anger, "Hanuman, did you get a chance to look around the city of Lanka."

Hanuman then went on to narrate how he burnt the golden Lanka, destroyed Ravana's palace and brought about enormous devastation in the city.

Rama sat quietly on a rock near the shore watching the dancing waves of the ocean. As he looked up, he saw Lanka in the distance looking like a tiny *speck*[2].

Suddenly Rama felt something *stir*[3] behind him. As he turned around he saw Sugriva and Vibhishana coming towards him. Vibhishana, the younger brother of Ravana, had *defected*[4] Ravana and joined Rama in the war.

"I cannot understand how we will reach Lanka? It seems I'll never be able to rescue Sita," Rama said sadly.

Vibhishana said softly, "Why don't you seek help from the ocean?"

2. *speck – dot*   4. *defected – deserted*
3. *stir – move*

Rama *invoked*[5] the Ocean God with folded palms, "O dear lord, master of the waves, we seek you, bless us with your mighty presence. Stop your waves so that we may be able to build a safe passage across your waters."

"You may make a bridge here to cross the ocean. I will make a passage for your bridge. Nala, one of your generals, is the son of divine architect Vishwakarma. Ask him to build a bridge across me and I will hold it up. This is the only way in which I can help you," Ocean God told Rama and *vanished*[6].

Thus the building of the bridge began. The monkeys uprooted the trees and collected huge *boulders*[7]. They jumped up and down and brought rocks to the shore. They were shouting and *squealing*[8] with happiness and worked swiftly with *enthusiasm*[9].

Even small animals ran about with tiny pieces of wood or stone in their mouths treading the paths shown by the eagles.

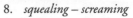

5. *invoked – called upon*
6. *vanished – gone*
7. *boulders – rock*

8. *squealing – screaming*
9. *enthusiasm – zeal*

Hanuman chanted the magic *mantra* over each boulder. As the monkeys threw the giant boulders in the ocean, the water *splashed*[10] high up in the air.

The work went on with great speed. The bridge was a hundred *yojan* long and ten *yojan* wide. The entire bridge was constructed in five days.

Rama *inaugurated*[11] the bridge and set out to cross the ocean. Lakshmana followed him, then Sugriva, and the rest of the monkey army followed them dancing with joy. The ocean held its breath while the entire army of Rama crossed the ocean.

---

10. *splashed – streaked*   11. *inaugurated – launched*

An Understanding

Q & A

Q. What did Hanuman give to Rama?

Ans. _____

_____

Q. Who defected and came into Rama's camp from Ravana's kingdom?

Ans. _____

_____

Q. Whom did Rama invoke in order to build the bridge to Lanka?

_____

_____

Q. What did the Ocean God say to Rama?

Ans. _____

_____

Q. In how many days was the bridge built?

Ans. _____

_____

Who & Whom

Who said this and to whom?

1. "I met her. She is well, but is a prisoner in Ravana's palace garden, Ashok Vatika. She only thinks of you and has been fasting. She asked me to give you this."

_____

_____

2. "You may make a bridge here to cross the ocean. I will make a passage for your bridge. Nala, one of your generals, is the son of divine architect Vishwakarma. Ask him to build a bridge across me and I will hold it up. This is the only way in which I can help you."

_____

_____

3. "Why don't you seek help from the ocean?"

_____

_____

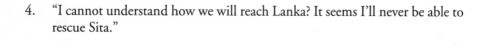

4. "I cannot understand how we will reach Lanka? It seems I'll never be able to rescue Sita."

_____

_____

Food for Thought

Imagine yourself to be a monkey in Rama's army who is helping in building the bridge. Write a diary entry of the day describing your feelings about the bridge and the close association of the monkey army with Lord Rama.

Life Skills

In Ramayana, bridges of stone were made. In modern times, we build different types of bridges like cantilever bridge, suspended bridge, beam bridge, arch bridge, etc. Visit the Internet site and learn more about different types of bridges.

22

The Great Fight

At night, Rama's army camped on the shore of the ocean. The morning dawned and bugles sounded the war-cry. In a final attempt, Rama sent Angada to *pursuade*[1] Ravana to surrender without a war. But Ravana refused. Now Rama and his army had no choice but to fight. The first day saw a duel between Ravana and Sugriva. As the day ended, the demons felt disappointed with the result of the fight.

The next day, as Indrajit, Ravana's son stood watching the war, he realised that the demon army was losing more soldiers than the monkeys. In panic, he used

---

1. *persuade – convince*

the serpent-arrow on Rama and Lakshmana. Rama and Lakshmana felt two slimy serpents wrapped around their legs and making way up towards their throats. Rama and Lakshmana began to lose consciousness and fell to the ground. They could not move any part of their body. Their physician Susena asked Hanuman to bring some herbs. As Hanuman was getting ready to go to Chandra and Drona mountains, a miracle happened.

An *enormous*[2], magnificent eagle named Garuda, the feathered vehicle of Vishnu, descended on the shores of Lanka. Garuda fluttered his wings and the serpents *scurried*[3] away leaving Rama and Lakshmana unconscious.

When Rama and Lakshmana came to their senses, they enquired about the eagle. To this, Garuda bowed his head and said, "I'm Garuda. I've broken the serpents' spell which was put on you by Indrajit." Saying this he fluttered his huge wings and flew heavenwards.

The fighting went on. As and when Ravana heard of the death of his most loyal and brave generals, he jumped with *fury*[4].

2. *enormous – massive*
3. *scurried – rushed*

4. *fury – rage*

"It's about time we woke up Kumbhakarna," he ordered his generals, "wake up my brother Kumbhakarna. He is needed here now."

Kumbhakarna was huge in size. Kumbhakarna had been cursed which caused him to sleep for six months in a year. He remained awake for the rest of the six months. This was the time when he slept, so it was practically impossible to wake him up till he slept for complete six months. It was only nine days that he had gone into *slumber*[5]. With great difficulty, the demons managed to wake him up.

Kumbhakarana fought well in the battlefield. Rama knew that the ordinary arrows would be useless against such a huge demon. He thought for a while then decided to use the magic weapons which Sage Vishwamitra had taught him to summon.

First of all Rama invoked Vayu's weapon and severed Kumbhakarna's right arm. Then invoking Indra's weapon Rama cut off Kumbhakarna's other arm. His *mutilated*[6] limbs were bleeding profusely and fountains of blood sprang from them, but Kumbhakarna seemed little perturbed with them. He laughed out loud as he drew closer to Rama.

---

5. *slumber – snooze*   6. *mutilated – maimed*

Then Rama shut his eyes and said a silent prayer summoning more divine weapons to kill Kumbhakarna.

A golden-tipped arrow came from nowhere and settled itself into Rama's bow. He shot the arrow directly at the Kumbhakarna's head. The arrow sliced his head off.

Kumbhakarna's head, which was still roaring with laughter, shot up into the sky and then fell on the highest *citadel* in Lanka and burst into flames. His massive body collapsed into the ocean crushing the sea creatures underneath as it buried itself on the ocean bed. The earth shook and the heaven rejoiced as Kumbhakarna was killed.

7. *Citadel – Fortress*

An Understanding

Q & A

Q. Who dueled with Ravana on the first day of the battle?

Ans. _____

_____

Q. Which spell was used by Indrajit on Rama and Lakshmana?

Ans. _____

_____

Q. Who countered that spell and how?

Ans. _____

_____

Q. Who was Kumbhakarna?

Ans. _____

_____

Q. What happened to Kumbhakarna in the end?

Ans. _____

_____

Common Error & Correction

There is one grammatical error in each of these sentences. Edit the error by first underlining it and then writing the corrected sentence

1. Kumbhakarna had been curse which caused him to sleep for six months in a year.

_____

_____

2. Garuda fluttered his wings and the serpents scurried away leave unconscious Rama and Lakshmana.

_____

_____

3. I has broken the serpents' spell which was put on you by Indrajit.

_____

_____

4. They could not moves any part of their body.

_____

_____

5. The first days saw a dual between Ravana and Sugriva.

_____

_____

Food for Thought

Write the dialogues between the following using your imagination.
The topic is 'Death of Kumbhakarna'.

- Ravana and his wife Mandodari
- Indrajit and his army commander
- Rama and Sugriva

Life Skills

'Kumbhakarna' has become synonymous to 'sleep'. Even today when someone oversleeps, we call him Kumbhakarna. Find out four more such characters from mythology or any other literature that have become synonymous to some activity in our daily life.

23

Sanjeevani Booti

Ravana had lost his brave sons in this battle. He was sad beyond expression. This was a *ruthless*[1] battle in which he proved to be the loser. But he would not lose hope. He would never return Sita – at least not now. Not after so much *bloodshed*[2]. It was a matter of his pride. He, the mightiest of all, must win this battle.

Ravana's thoughts were interrupted by his son Indrajit's voice. He was standing before him, dressed to go to the battlefield.

"I've come to take your blessings father. I'm going to take revenge from Rama for killing my brothers. Do not *despair*[3]. I promise you that I will come to you with the heads of Rama and Lakshmana." Indrajit bowed his head before Ravana.

Indrajit took to the battle with a fiery *fervor*[4]. He began attacking the monkey army. His sky-rocketing roars were enough to send a person running with fear. This is the reason Indrajit was also known as Meghnad. Lakshmana set out to kill Indrajit .

Lakshmana targeted Indrajit and shot a *volley*[5] of arrows at him like rays of brightness coming from the Sun. Indrajit shot back and soon a mighty battle *ensued*[6] between the two brave warriors. Sensing that he could not win in a fair game, Indrajit again resorted to magic. He used his most powerful weapon *Brahmastra* against Lakshmana before retreating for the night.

Lakshmana fell down unconscious. The monkeys surrounded Lakshmana. Rama sat down beside him overcome with grief.

Vibhishana called the physician Sushena who checked Lakshmana and then said to Vibhishana, "He is not dead. He has been hit by *Brahmastra* for which the only cure is a special herb called *Sanjeevani booti*. It is a combination of four herbs. It grows in the Himalayas."

"But the Himalayas is not here. It is very far off. Who will bring this herb from there?" wondered Vibhishana.

"I'll go there," Hanuman offered. "Just tell me what this herb looks like. I'll bring it for you."

---

1. *ruthless – cruel*
2. *bloodshed – slaughter*
3. *despair – anguish*

4. *fervor – zeal*
5. *volley – stream*
6. *ensued – follow*

Sushena said, "Go to the Himalayas and bring the herbs which glow brightly. There are special lights *emanating*[7] from them. But we need these herbs before sunrise tomorrow and the Himalayas is a long way from here. Do you think you will be able to do it?"

Hanuman said firmly, "I'll do anything for my Lord Rama. I shall be here with them before dawn tomorrow."

Hanuman flew towards the Himalayas with the speed of wind. Soon he reached the Himalaya mountain.

As he stood at the hill amidst the herbs, he was in a state of dilemma. The entire hill was full of brilliant herbs with lights emanating from all of them. He could not recognise the herbs, Sushana had asked for. The time was running out. Hanuman

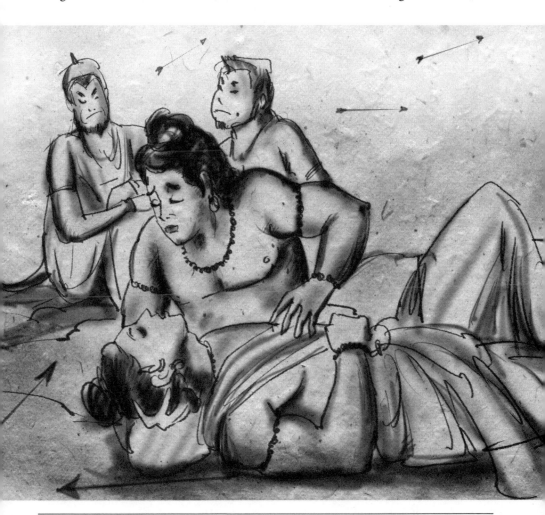

---

7. *emanating – radiating*

had to make a quick decision. Hanuman *pondered*[8] for a while then he decided to carry the entire hill with him.

Satisfied with his decision, Hanuman lifted the entire hill of herbs and left for Lanka at the speed of lightning.

The dawn was just breaking. All the anxious monkeys awaited his arrival outside their camp. Rama sat beside Lakshmana who was still *sprawled*[9] unconscious on the ground. The soothing aroma of the herbs *revived*[10] Lakshmana. He opened his eyes. Rama embraced his dear brother.

The night of terror had passed. Lakshmana had come back from the clutches of death.

---

8. *pondered – thought about*   10. *revived – invigorated*
9. *sprawled – lay down*

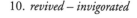

An Understanding

Q & A

Q. Why was Ravana angry?

Ans. _____

_____

Q. Who promised to take revenge from Rama?

Ans. _____

_____

Q. How did Indrajit injure Lakshmana?

Ans. _____

_____

Q. What did Sushena ask Hanuman to bring?

Ans. _____

_____

Q. Why was Hanuman confused when he reached the Himalaya mountain?

Ans. _____

_____

Common Error & Correction

Rewrite these sentences by correcting both, the grammar and facts

1. Ravana was beside herself with joy on losing his brave daughters in the battle.

_____

_____

2. Indrajit promised to coming back with heads of Sita and Urmila for Ravana.

_____

_____

3. Indrajit shot bake and soon a mighty battle starting between him and Rama.

_____

_____

4. Hanuman flown towards Himalaya with the speed of a snail.

   _____

   _____

5. Hanuman carried the entire pond with her.

   _____

   _____

Food for Thought

Do you think bloodshed, fighting, and hatred are good for any race or civilization? Pen down your views about it in about 50 words.

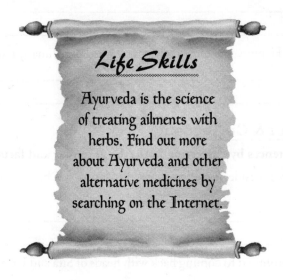

Life Skills

Ayurveda is the science of treating ailments with herbs. Find out more about Ayurveda and other alternative medicines by searching on the Internet.

have been the *yuvraj* of Ayodhya and my father would have been alive. But I will amend things now. I am going to the forest to bring back brother Rama. Get the army ready. We shall bring him back to his coronation with the *splendour*[2] of a crown prince that he truly deserves."

Saying so, Bharata left the court leaving no place for discussion.

The journey to Sage Bhardwaj's ashram was smooth and full of delight as Bharata was very excited to meet his brothers.

While at Chitrakoot, Lakshmana was guarding the cottage which Rama, Sita, and Lakshmana had made their home for fourteen years.

When Bharata and his *convoy*[3] reached the cottage, they found Rama, Lakshmana, and Sita standing outside waiting for them.

Bharata fell at Rama's feet, "Please forgive me. It was because of my mother that you are living in this condition. I beg you to return at once to Ayodhya and take your

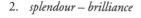
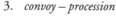

2. *splendour – brilliance*   3. *convoy – procession*

rightful place on the throne of Ayodhya."

Then he gave the news of the *demise*[4] of their father to Rama and Lakshmana. Rama stood very still. His face showed no emotion, but the turmoil in his heart could be clearly seen. Lakshmana fell down on the floor on hearing the news and started to cry.

After a long time, when Rama and Lakshmana had come to terms with their father's departure to heaven, Bharata once again *broached*[5] the subject of Rama coming back to Ayodhya and taking over as king.

But Rama would hear none of it. "A promise is a promise," Rama said, "I will not return to Ayodhya until fourteen years have elapsed. Bharata, you must return to Ayodhya and be a great king, like our father."

But Bharata was equally *adamant*[6]. He begged Rama like a child, "I will stay in the forest instead," he offered. All the three brothers offered to live in the forest to

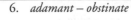

4. *demise – death*
5. *broached – mentioned*

6. *adamant – obstinate*

fulfil their father's wish and convoy let Rama go back to Ayodhya. But nothing could shake Rama's *resolve*[7]. His father's word was of utmost importance to him, especially now that he was no more.

Finally Bharata had to accept the fact that Rama would not go back. He said, "Next to our father, you are my father. Your wish is my command and I have to fulfil it."

"I'll rule" he declared, "but only in your name. I will not sit on the throne. I will make sure that your kingdom is safe, but I will not be the king. I will not live in the palace, but in a small hut like yours till you come back and take back your kingdom from me. Till then, I shall take your *khadaun*[8] with me. I shall place them on the throne. They will symbolise your presence and rule over Ayodhya till the day you return."

As the sun set, they made the most of what they knew would be their last hour together in many... many years to come. As they departed, Bharata carried Rama's *khadaun* with him and his picture in his heart.

---

7. *resolve –determination*   8. *khadaun – sandals*

An Understanding

Q & A

Q. Who performed the last rites of King Dasharatha?

Ans. _____

_____

Q. How did Bharata react to his mother's devious plot?

Ans. _____

_____

Q. Why did Bharata decide to go to the forest?

Ans. _____

_____

Q. What did Bharata say to Rama when he met him in the forest?

Ans. _____

_____

Q. Why did Bharata bring Rama's *khadaun* with him?

Ans. _____

_____

Fill in the blanks

1. .... and ....were called from their maternal grandfather's house.

2. Bharata was angry at his mother, Kaikeyi's ....plot.

3. Rama and Lakshmana had built a hut at.............

4. ....fell down on the floor on hearing the news of their father's demise and started to cry.

5. Bharata carried Rama's ....with him to Ayodhya.

Comprehension

Rewrite the story of Bharata and Rama's reunion with the help of these keywords

- ➤ *Khadaun*
- ➤ Rama's hut
- ➤ Chitrakoot
- ➤ A promise is a promise
- ➤ Bid farewell
- ➤ Father's demise
- ➤ Bharata's convoy

_____

_____

_____

_____

_____

_____

_____

_____

_____

_____

_____

_____

_____

_____

_____

_____

_____

_____

_____

_____

_____

Food for Thought

When Lakshmana saw Bharata coming in with a huge army, he assumed that Bharata was coming to kill them. What would have happened if he had attacked Bharata's army immediately without consulting Rama? Write a battle scene based on the above assumption describing the way Rama and Bharata would react to Lakshmana's unthoughtful action.

Life Skills

Bharata displayed brotherly love when he announced himself to be an envoy of Rama to the throne of Ayodhya.
Such incidents of modesty are not common in life.
But true value of relations can still be enjoyed if we learn to give more than we take from others.

Aranya Kand

Forest Retreat

Rama, Sita, and Lakshmana enter the great Dandaka Forest and adore the eminent sages, who are in penance and hermitages in that forest. This Kand is named Aranya Kanda not just to show that Rama just roamed in forests. The forests, as per Indian tradition, are the treasure houses of knowledge, and they are the ultimate in Vedic culture.

Ravana, though persuaded by Mareecha not to encounter Rama, refused to listen to any advise and went ahead to abduct Sita.

Rama did much good in Aranya Kand in wiping out those greedy, dictatorial, magically-overpowering creatures called *rakshasas*. In fact, in Aranya Kand, Rama did more social work than miracles. Hence the sociological pursuits of Rama led to the establishment of one great orderly civil empire under one emperor, that later came to be known as *Rama Rajya*.

Further, it is said that Rama killed these *rakshasas* in thousands, which brings to mind as to how can an archer eliminate thousands of *rakshasas*, with just a bow and arrow. It may not be surprising that when a single trigger can create havoc of Hiroshima or Nagasaki, then in all probability Rama also might have triggered a missile-like weapon in the same way, through the weapons given to him by Sage Vishwamitra.

Panchvati

As Bharata left for Ayodhya, Rama decided to move deeper into the Dandaka forest. Though Chitrakoot was a lovely place, still he felt restless because memories of Bharata and the news of Dasharatha's death made him *restive*[1].

First they went to Sage Atri's hermitage. Sage Atri and his wife Anusuya welcomed them with affection. After spending a pleasant night there, Rama, Sita, and Lakshmana moved on.

---

1. *restive – restless*

Soon they came across the hermitage of Sage Sutikshna. He was a *disciple*[2] of Sage Agastya. He welcomed Rama, Sita, and Lakshmana with open arms. Later in the day, as they sat down after a meal, Sage Sutikshna told Rama about the demons and the *atrocities*[3] committed by them. He also asked them to go and meet his *guru*, Sage Agastya in his *ashram* which was nearby.

When they arrived at the hermitage of Sage Agastya they were taken to the honourable sage by his disciples. Agastya blessed Rama, Sita, and Lakshmana and welcomed them heartily. He treated them as his honoured guests, serving them food that was appropriate for *ascetics*[4].

Rama thanked Sage Agastya and asked him about a place where they could settle down and live in peace.

2. *disciple – follower*
3. *atrocities – violence*

4. *ascetics – hermits*

Sage Agastya thought for a while and said, "There is one such place which is not very far from here. This place is close to the river Godavari, so there is abundant water and vegetation there. It is home to different kinds of animals. It is called Panchvati. You will find it a pleasant place to live in."

Next day, Rama, Sita, and Lakshmana bade their farewell to the sage and set off towards Panchvati.

As they walked on, the path began to climb up. Soon they came to a beautiful hilly area. They had reached Panchvati. Its scenic beauty captured their imagination. They were charmed by the beauty and the *sanctity*[5] of Panchvati. The air was cool and fresh. There was fragrance of flowers in the *breeze*[6]. They could see a river *glistening*[7] around the hills.

Beautiful deer and other animals were seen drinking water on the banks of the river. Tall trees grew in *abundance*[8]. Shrubs of fragrant flowers surrounded the grassy *meadow*[9].

"This is where we should live," said Rama, while Sita and Lakshmana nodded in agreement.

Lakshmana quickly built a lovely hut and soon they settled down in Panchvati. Life in Panchvati was peaceful. A routine set in their lives. They would get up early in the morning and bathe in the river Godavari. Then they would gather flowers and offer prayers to the Sun God. After that they would drink the fresh cool water from the spring and eat whatever fruits and berries they could gather. They would tend to the hut and look after the animals that came by. As time went by, Rama, Sita, and Lakshmana grew *spiritually*[10]. Living amidst the sages, they learnt meditation and prayer. They were now stronger in spirit as well as in body.

Time passed slowly but happily. Sita could hardly remember her old life in the palace. The soft bed, the silken robes, the shining jewels, and the delicious foods – all seemed very far and unreal. Panchvati was her home now. She was happy here as she got to spend so much more time with her husband.

---

5. *sanctity – purity*
6. *breeze – gentle wind*
7. *glistening – shiny*
8. *abundance – plenty*
9. *meadow – pasture*
10. *spiritually – morally*

An Understanding

Q & A

Q. Why did Rama move away from Chitrakoot?

Ans. _____

_____

Q. Who was the disciple of Sage Agastya?

Ans. _____

_____

Q. Who sent Rama, Sita, and Lakshmana to Panchvati?

Ans. _____

_____

Q. Describe the life in Panchvati?

Ans. _____

_____

_____

Q. How did Rama, Sita, and Lakshmana grow spiritually at Panchvati?

Ans. _____

_____

Comprehension

Describe the beauty of Panchvati in your own words

_____

_____

_____

_____

_____

_____

Food for Thought

Why do you think Sita was happier in the forest than
she was in the palace?

Life Skills

Visit a forested area with
your parents and enjoy the
scenic beauty of that place.
Describe how life in that
place would be different
from the city life.

11

Soorpanakha

Years rolled by. Sita had made friends with deer and monkeys, and rabbits and squirrels, who came to visit her every day. The forest always had something new to offer to them. But this peaceful life was not to last. The evil eyes watched them from the *bewilderness*[1] of the forest.

Soorpanakha was the sister of demon king Ravana. She roamed in the forest hunting for wild animals. One day, as Soorpanakha was passing by their hut, she saw Rama sitting outside his hut.

---

1. *bewilderness – wild*

She fell in love with him. "What a handsome man. I cannot live without him. I must marry him."

Immediately she changed herself into a beautiful woman and went to Rama. "O handsome! I'm Princess Soorpanakha. I'm the sister of Ravana, the great king of Lanka. What are you doing here in this wild? Come with me. We will get married and live in a palace. I'll provide you all the pleasures you want." She *fluttered*[2] her eyelashes so as to charm the handsome Rama.

Rama was surprised but he spoke gently, "Lady, I cannot marry you. You see, I'm already married. She is my wife." He pointed towards Sita who was sitting nearby. "But look, there is my brother who is younger to me and more handsome than I am. You can ask him if he would like to marry you," said Rama, laughing.

Soorpanakha turned towards Lakshmana who was watching the whole scene with a naughty smile on his face.

"All right. I'll marry him. Come, let's go."

2. *fluttered – flapped*

As she laid a hand on his arm, Lakshmana pushed her away, "No way. I cannot come with you. I am the servant of my brother. Why do you want to marry a slave like me and become a slave yourself? Go and try your luck with my brother."

Soorpanakha went back to Rama who again *declined*[3] her offer. This process went on for some time when suddenly Soorpanakha lost her temper. "This woman is the root cause of all problem. I will eat her up then you can marry me."

Her beautiful face turned an ugly shade and her hands *sprouted*[4] into claws. She reached out to *grab*[5] Sita's hand.

Rama realised that she was a demoness. Instantly he sprang up and called out to Lakshmana, "You deal with her I am taking Sita into the hut."

Lakshmana pulled out his dagger with a lightning movement and cut off Soorpanakha's nose and the tips of her long hairy ears.

Soorpanakha screamed in pain as blood dripped from her nose and ears. She covered her face and ran into the forest, screaming, "Wait till I tell my brothers what you did to me. I will make you pay for this insult. They will take *revenge*[6] from you."

Her screams shattered the peace and quiet of Panchvati. As she went away, everyone heaved a sigh of relief. Little did they know that Soorpanakha's scream marked the end of the peaceful *rhythm*[7] of their days altogether. This was just the beginning of a long period of *turmoil*[8] during which Rama would have to fight many battles and Sita would have to suffer quietly.

---

3. *declined – refused*
4. *sprouted – grew*
5. *grab – grasp*

6. *revenge – vengeance*
7. *rhythm – beat*
8. *turmoil – chaos*

An Understanding

Q & A

Q. Who was Soorpanakha?

Ans. _____

_____

Q. Why did she go to Rama?

Ans. _____

_____

Q. Why did Rama send her to Lakshmana?

Ans. _____

_____

Q. What did Lakshmana tell Soorpanakha?

Ans. _____

_____

Q. Why did Lakshmana cut Soorpanakha's nose and ears?

Ans. _____

_____

Fill in the blanks

1. Soorpanakha fell in love with………..
2. Rama pointed towards ………who was sitting nearby.
3. Both Rama and Lakshmana declined Soorpanakha's offer of ……………
4. Lakshmana cut Soorpanakha's……………and…………….
5. Soorpanakha's screams shattered the peace and quiet of………….

Life-sketch

Prepare a life-sketch of Soorpanakha in about 30-40 words.

_____

_____

_____

Food for Thought

Rama and Lakshmana should not have made fun of Soorpanakha
by sending her to and fro. Do you agree?
Give reasons for your answer.

Life Skills

Cosmetic surgery is much in
vogue today. If Soorpanakha
was born in modern times, she
could have got her nose and
ears repaired with cosmetic
surgery. However, Sushruta,
the famous ancient surgeon, is
also known to have specialised
in cosmetic surgery. Find out
more about
the contribution of Sushruta to
the field of medicine.

12

Sita's Abduction

Soorpanakha ran straight to her stepbrothers Khara and Dushana and gave them her own *version*[1] of what happened.

"I was wandering in the forest when I saw three humans. I went up to ask them what they were doing in our forest where no one dares to enter. But as soon as they saw me, they chopped off my nose and my ears. Oh, how it hurts, brother," she

---

1. *version – account*

howled, "just two frail humans and see what they have done to your sister. You must take revenge on my behalf. Save our honour by punishing them for this *horrendous*[2] deed."

Accompanied by their army, Khara and Dushana went to Panchvati to take revenge from Rama and Lakshmana but fell to their end.

Then Soorpanakha went to her brother, demon king Ravana and told him the same story.

Ravana ruled over the rich kingdom of Lanka. The entire Lanka was made of gold. Ravana's palace was made of solid gold, with diamond and ruby pillars and emerald-*studded*[3] walls. He wore ten crowns, one on each head. Each crown was *lavishly*[4] decorated with rubies, diamonds, sapphires emeralds, and pearls. Though Ravana was a powerful king still he was neither just nor noble. He was selfish and proud.

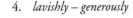

2. *horrendous – dreadful*   4. *lavishly – generously*
3. *studded – attached*

After listening to everything from Soorpanakha, Ravana decided to use his brain rather than might and defeat Rama.

"I'll give Rama a piece of his own mind. I'll strike his honour just like he did mine by hurting my sister. I'll carry off Rama's wife. That will harm him more than any army can do." Ravana declared.

It was a cool, bright morning. Sita was gathering flowers from her garden for their morning prayers. Just as Sita turned to go back to the hut, she saw a golden deer standing at a corner of their hut. Leaving her flower basket there, Sita ran towards the edge of the hut where she saw the golden deer.

Sita looked at Rama pleadingly, "Please catch that deer for me. I'll keep it as a pet. We will take it back to Ayodhya."

Mareecha, in the *disguise*[5] of the golden deer, was waiting for Rama a little ahead. Playing hide and seek, Mareecha led Rama deep into the forest far away from his

---

5. *disguise – cover up*

cottage, then he cried out in a voice that was exactly like Rama's "O Lakshmana….
O Sita!"

Lakshmana and Sita both heard Rama's voice. Sita forced Lakshmana to go to the
forest in search of Rama. At first Lakshmana refused to leave her alone in the hut but on
Sita's *insistence*[6] he said, "I'm going into the forest, but listen to me carefully, I will draw
you a holy line – *Lakshmana Rekha* – and I beg of you to not to cross this line till any of
us comes back. So long as you are in it, you will be safe. If anyone else tries to cross this
line, that person will be burnt to ashes."

As soon as Lakshmana left, Ravana in the disguise of a hermit arrived at Sita's
doorstep. "Alms for the hermit! O kind lady, please give something to this hermit."

Sita went inside her hut and brought some fruits and berries on a leaf. She placed
them outside the *Lakshmana Rekha* and stayed inside.

Ravana refused to even touch the offering in this way. "I'm not a beggar. Come
out here and give the alms respectfully in my hands."

At first Sita hesitated, but then she picked up the leaf and walked out of the
Lakshmana Rekha to give the fruits to the old hermit.

Lightning flashed, thunder roared, and the *Lakshmana Rekha* itself burst into
flames. Sita tried to step back but Ravana, in the disguise of hermit, stepped forward
and grabbed her hand. As he touched her, his disguise disappeared and his ten heads
danced like hooded cobras.

Sita tried to pull back but Ravana's grip was firm. She started chanting Rama's name.
Ravana gave a thundering cry of rage and grabbed her by the hair. In a flash he pulled her into
his chariot, Pushpak Vimana. The chariot rose high up in the sky.

"Rama…O Rama, help me! Lakshmana…Lakshmana…help me!" Sita cried but
neither Rama nor Lakshmana could hear her cry.

6. *insistence – persistence*

An Understanding

Q & A

Q. Whom did Soorpanakha approach first?

Ans. _____

_____

Q. Who was Ravana?

Ans. _____

_____

Q. Whom did Ravana send in the form of a golden deer?

Ans. _____

_____

Q. Why did the old hermit refuse to take the alms from Sita?

Ans. _____

_____

Q. What happened when Sita crossed the *Lakshmana-Rekha*?

Ans. _____

_____

Yes or No

1. Soorpanakha was Ravana's sister.   ___
2. Sita wanted to keep the golden deer as her pet. ___
3. Lakshmana drew a *Rama Rekha* around the hut.   ___
4. Ravana came in the form of a golden deer.   ___
5. Ravana grabbed Sita's hand.   ___

Comprehension

Describe Ravana's Lanaka and his wealth in 20–30 words

_____

_____

_____

Food for Thought

If Sita had not come out of the *Lakshmana Rekha*, the story of
Ramayana would have been different. Explain how?

Life Skills

Lakshmana Rekha is
symbol of a protective
shield or space provided to
our loved ones. Recall any
such incident when you
felt protected by your loved
ones in the same manner.

In Search of Sita

13

When Rama and Lakshmana came back to the hut, they were *distraught*[1] at not seeing Sita there. The hut was strangely quiet. A broken leaf plate, berries, and roots lay scattered outside the circle Lakshmana had drawn for Sita. They moved out in search of Sita. On the way they found Sita's ornaments lying on the ground.

They walked on further until Lakshmana suddenly stopped. He had spotted

---

1. *distraught – distressed*

something in the nearby bushes. He motioned Rama to stop and himself went closer to the bushes. It was a broken wheel of a chariot. The two brothers looked at the wheel when suddenly Rama saw a *clump*[2] of torn feathers dripping with blood lying near the trunk of the tree.

Suddenly Rama heard a sharp cry of pain.

It was Jatayu. The old bird lay there *severely*[3] wounded counting his last breaths.

"Come closer, my dear Rama, I do not have much time left," he whispered painfully, "I tried to save Sita, but Ravana, the king of Lanka, carried her away in his chariot – *Pushpak Viman*... I fought with him...but... he cut off my wings...Go... Rama...hurry...save her." With one last painful gasp, Jatayu breathed his last.

After cremating Jatayu, Rama and Lakshmana walked on without a hint as to where they could find Ravana. On the way they met Kabandha, a *celestial*[4] creature stuck in the body of demon due to a curse given to him by Sage Sthulashiras. Kabandha was glad on getting *salvation*[5] when Rama shot him with the golden arrow. Before he departed to heaven, he advised Rama, "Go to Pampa Lake. There is a monkey king named Sugriva who was displaced by his brother Bali, the son of Indra. He lives on the Rishyamukha mountain. He will help you get Sita back. He is brave and able. He will search the river, mountains, and the deep caves with his monkey army and help you find your wife."

Kabandha explained in *minute*[6] details the directions to reach the exact spot where Sugriva lived. Then he folded his hands and bid farewell to Rama. His chariot flew up and disappeared among the high clouds.

It was getting dark. Rama and Lakshmana were tired from the long journey. They were heading towards Pampa Lake in search of Sugriva as suggested by Kabandha. They saw a hermitage before them. They decided to break their journey and take some rest. It was the hermitage of Shabari who was famous Sage Matanga's disciple.

Hearing some noises, Shabari came out of the hut. She was pleasantly surprised to see Rama and Lakshmana at the door. She was aged but she recognised Rama instantly. She was *overwhelmed*[7] with joy.

She ran to fetch some water to wash Rama's lotus feet. With great devotion she cleaned his feet and then took them both inside the hut.

"My lord, you must be hungry," saying so, old Shabari went inside in search of some food, but all that she could find in the hut were some berries. She quickly washed them and brought them to Rama and Lakshmana.

---

2. *clump – cluster*
3. *severely – cruelly*
4. *celestial – divine*

5. *salvation – escape*
6. *minute – tiny*
7. *overwhelmed – inundated*

She took a bite from one berry. It was sweet. She handed it over to Rama, who took it from her and ate it with a smile on his face.. Then she tasted another one. It was bitter. She threw it away. In this way, she went on tasting each and every berry and handed over the sweet ones to Rama and Lakshmana. While Rama was eating those berries gladly, Lakshmana could not bear to put even one berry in his mouth. As Shabari went inside to bring some more berries, Lakshmana told Rama, "Brother, this woman is a fool. She is first eating them and then giving the same berries to you to eat. How can you eat her half-eaten berries? Permit me; I will give her a good scolding[8]. Is this any way to treat your guests?"

At this Rama smiled and said, "Lakshmana, you only saw the half-eaten berries but you did not see her devotion. She wants only the best for us that is why she is tasting the berries first and giving us only the sweet berries while throwing away the bitter ones. She is my true devotee who has only my welfare in mind."

---

8. *scolding – rebuke*

This made Lakshmana realise the truth. Then on he too did not hesitate in eating the half-eaten berries offered by old Shabari.

After resting for a while, Rama and Lakshmana got ready to carry on with their journey. Before leaving, Rama enquired about Sita from Shabari. He also told her about Kabandh and his suggestion to team up with Sugriva.

"He gave you the right advice. Go to Sugriva. He is a noble being. He will certainly help you find Sita," Shabari assured Rama.

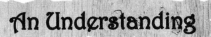

An Understanding

Q & A

Q. Why were Rama and Lakshmana distraught at coming back to the hut?

Ans. _____

_____

Q. What did Jatayu tell Rama?

Ans. _____

_____

Q. Who was Kabandha?

Ans. _____

_____

Q. What advise did Kabandha give to Rama?

Ans. _____

_____

Q. Why did Lakshmana want to scold Shabari?

Ans. _____

_____

Who & Whom

Who said this to whom?

1. "Brother, this woman is a fool. She is first eating them and then giving the same berries to you to eat. "

_____

_____

2. "I tried to save Sita, but Ravana, the king of Lanka, carried her away in his chariot…"

_____

_____

3. "He gave you the right advice. Go to Sugriva. He is a noble being. He will certainly help you find Sita."

_____

_____

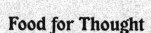

Food for Thought

How did Jatayu help Rama in his search for Sita?

Life Skills

Rama gave a different perspective to Shabari's half-eaten berries. Choose any two situations in your real life which you can present in two different perspectives.

Kishkindha Kand

Grandeur of Alliance

Rama, in his search for Sita, reaches Pampa Lake along with Lakshmana. Rama visualises Pampa Lake as a heavenly abode and narrates to Lakshmana the suffering he is undergoing due to the departure of Sita.

The area of Pampa Lake is compared to heavens and its trees and birds with divine souls. The fragrant breeze metaphors with god's gift, flowers as pure knowledge, and the tranquil water as clear heart.

In this Kand, Rama meets Hanuman and Sugriva. Rama forms an alliance with Sugriva that he would help Sugriva kill Bali and in return Sugriva would help him find Sita.

Later Rama deputes Hanuman to find Sita. Hanuman is in a dilemma whether he will be able to perform such a gigantic task of crossing the ocean. Jambavan reminds Hanuman of his immense strength. Hanuman takes Rama's ring as a token. He climbs up the top of Mahendra Mountain and gets ready to take a leap across the ocean.

14

Rama–Sugriva Alliance

"Hanuman, I see someone coming towards Rishyamukha mountain," Sugriva called out to Hanuman who was sitting beside him. He felt scared. Even from the distance he could make out that the two visitors were well-armed. The suspicion rose in his heart and fear gripped him.

Was it another of Bali's *ploys*[1] to get him killed? Sugriva was hiding in Rishyamukha mountain in fear of his elder brother Bali who had taken away his kingdom and his

---

1. *ploy – plan*

wife *deceptively*[2]. He sent Hanuman to find out about the two visitors.

Hanuman went to Rama in disguise of an old man and enquired about his whereabouts. Rama looked up and smiled at him. A smile from Rama evoked a strange sensation in Hanuman's heart. He changed back to his original form.

"My Lord," he said *reverently*[3], "I do not know who you are but your presence makes my heart fill with unknown joy. I am Hanuman. I belong to the monkey clan. I came here because my chief Sugriva wanted to know who you are and what you were doing here."

"He is Sugriva's minister," Rama said in delight to Lakshmana. "It is indeed fortunate that you have come to us, Hanuman. We have been looking for Sugriva. We need his help to find out my wife Sita who has been kidnapped by the king of demons, Ravana. Hanuman, can you take us to Sugriva."

Hanuman rose quickly and made himself as huge as a hill.

2. *deceptively – dishonestly*   3. *reverently – respectfully*

"Please sit on my shoulders. I will carry you both to my chief Sugriva," Hanuman said.

Sugriva was waiting for them on the Malaya Mountain. Hanuman introduced Rama and Lakshmana to Sugriva. After they exchanged their *woes*[4] with each other, Hanuman spoke, "Rama is wise and *resolute*[5], exceedingly brave and honourable. He has come to you for help. Rama and Lakshmana are here to make an *alliance*[6] with you. Treat them well, for they are the best among those who should be honoured."

Sugriva nodded, "I would be grateful to extend any kind of help you require. I would be thankful if you could help me regain my home and my family in return. Take my hand and let us enter into a firm alliance."

Rama took Sugriva's *outstretched*[7] hand and gripped it firmly.

Pleased with the alliance, Rama embraced Sugriva with affection, "I shall help you regain your lost glory. That's my promise to you."

Sugriva too replied with similar affection, "I, on my part, promise to bring your wife back. Whether she be in the highest heaven or the lowest hell, I shall bring her back for you. You can count on my word, Rama."

Sugriva's words comforted Rama. Regaining his natural composure, Rama said, "Thank you. We shall plan out a strategy for finding Sita but first we must deal with your brother, Bali."

Hanuman, meanwhile, gathered some wood and *kindled*[8] a fire. He worshipped it with flowers and then placed the blazing fire between Rama and Sugriva as a symbol of their alliance. The two of them walked around the fire to turn their new friendship into a long-lasting relationship.

---

4. *woes – miseries*
5. *resolute – firm*
6. *alliance – union*

7. *outstretched – extended*
8. *kindled – started*

An Understanding

Q & A

Q. Who saw Rama and Lakshmana coming towards the Rishyamukha Mountain?

Ans. _____

_____

Q. Who was Sugriva?

Ans. _____

_____

Q. How did Hanuman take Rama and Lakshmana to Sugriva?

Ans. _____

_____

Q. What promise did Rama give to Sugriva?

Ans. _____

_____

Q. How did Hanuman seal the alliance between Rama and Sugriva?

Ans. _____

_____

Comprehension

Write dialogues between Rama and Sugriva as they exchange their woes and agree to enter into an alliance

_____

_____

_____

_____

_____

_____

Food for Thought

Justify the alliance between Rama and Sugriva.

Life Skills

You must have heard of alliance between countries and armies. Find out about some famous alliances in history.

Rama Kills Bali

ishkindha was a beautiful place. When they reached the city, Rama and Lakshmana stayed back, hiding behind the trees. Sugriva alone went to the palace. Outside the gates, he let out a mighty roar and challenged Bali, "Bali, come out and fight. This is Sugriva and I have come to take revenge from you because you have been unjust. You took away my home and my family from me."

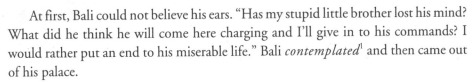

At first, Bali could not believe his ears. "Has my stupid little brother lost his mind? What did he think he will come here charging and I'll give in to his commands? I would rather put an end to his miserable life." Bali *contemplated*[1] and then came out of his palace.

Seeing Bali come out of the palace, Sugriva charged at him. The two brothers began to fight. Rama, who was hiding behind the tree, had his bow and arrow ready.

It was clear that Bali was stronger than Sugriva. Rama waited anxiously for the right moment. Just as Bali was about to *strangle*[2] Sugriva, Rama let go of the arrow. The arrow went flying straight to Bali's chest. Bali *collapsed*[3] to the ground.

Bali looked at Rama and then gently spoke those harsh words, which were critical of Rama's act, "You are famous for being just and truthful, why, then, did you shoot me in the back? How could someone like you, born a noble *kshatriya* in a noble family, do something so cruel? If you had shot me face to face, it would have been different,

---

1. *contemplated – thought*
2. *strangle – choke*

3. *collapsed – fell down*

but you never challenged me in the battle."

Rama looked at Bali and said in a gentle voice, "My dear Bali, you have not understood the true meaning of *dharma*[4]. You, yourself, have *transgressed*[5] the bounds of *dharma*. Your conduct is not appropriate of a ruler because you are driven entirely by pleasure. You have rejected the eternal *dharma* by taking away your brother's wife. Secondly, Sugriva is my friend and it is my duty to help my friend. I had promised to help Sugriva and it is against my *dharma* to go back on my word."

Rama's words opened Bali's eyes. Joining his palms together, he said to Rama, "You are right. I have received my right punishment. But before I go, I would like to request you to treat my son Angada and Sugriva alike. Also make sure that Sugriva is not harsh with my wife Tara. She has done nothing wrong. In fact, she was the one who always spoke in Sugriva's favour." With that the mighty king Bali lay dead on the ground.

Soon Sugriva was coronated as the king of Kishkindha. Sugriva was a just ruler. He made Bali's son Angad as *yuvraj*. Peace and order was restored to Kishkindha as the subjects accepted Sugriva as their king gladly.

---

4. *dharma – duty*   5. *transgressed – disobeyed*

An Understanding

Q & A

Q. Whom did Sugriva challenge to a duel?

Ans. _____

_____

Q. How did Rama help Sugriva in killing Bali?

Ans. _____

_____

Q. Why did Bali call Rama's act unjust?

Ans. _____

_____

Q. How had Bali transgressed from the path of *dharma*?

Ans. _____

_____

Q. What was Bali's last wish?

Ans. _____

_____

Complete the following sentences:

1. Sugriva alone went....................

2. Seeing Bali come out of the ....

3. Rama, who was hiding..................

4. Soon Sugriva was installed.................

5. He made Bali's son ....

6. Peace and order was................:..

Food for Thought

Was Rama justified in killing Bali in the name of fulfilling
a promise to help his friend Sugriva?

Life Skills

Is someone's promise more
important than life? Create
a situation akin to Bali's
killing in contemporary
times and then present
its solution according to
modern ideology.

Hanuman's Pursuit

The rainy season had begun. It was impossible for Rama and Lakshmana to continue their search for Sita. Rama grew sadder as the hope of finding Sita seemed dimmer with each passing day.

As soon as the monsoon season passed, Sugriva called the eight generals of his army including Nala, Angada, Hanuman, and Jambavana to *chart out*[1] their course of action. They mapped out their routes and divided the entire army in eight parts. "But how will we reach Lanka? If Ravana has crossed the seas with Sita, we have no

1. *chart out – prepare*

way to reach there," asked one of the generals in a worried manner.

"I'll go towards the south," said Hanuman, "I shall find a way to reach Lanka and look for her there."

Rama was overjoyed. He took off his ring, gave it to Hanuman and said, "Take this ring of mine. When you find Sita, tell her that you are my most valued messenger. Hanuman, I know in my heart you will be able to bring Sita back to me."

"How do I reach Lanka?" Hanuman wondered as he set off towards south.

When Hanuman and his army reached the ocean, the relief and excitement could be clearly seen on the faces of all the monkeys. They were quite excited to see the ocean.

But the big question was how to cross the ocean. Then they met Sampati, Jatayu's brother. When Hanuman gave him the news of his brother's demise, Sampati closed his eyes out of grief. When Sampati opened his eyes, they were blood shot with anger.

He looked sharply at Hanuman, "If Ravana has killed my brother, then I will help you find Ravana so that he can be killed. I have no wings so I cannot fly across the ocean, but over the years, my eyes have become sharp. I can see very far sitting here. Wait here, I will *hop*[2] to the high rock and look into Lanka to find about Sita." With this, he went away.

"I've seen her sitting in the Ashoka Vatika in the city of Lanka," Sampati announced gladly on his return. "Think of some way to get across the salty sea. You shall definitely find Sita where I told you. Your mission will soon be accomplished," saying so, Sampati flew away towards the *shore*[3], leaving the monkeys to plan their next move.

The morning dawned with new hope. But who would cross the ocean to go to Lanka? The question kept *haunting*[4] all the monkeys when Angada summoned them.

"I want to go to Lanka but I don't know whether I'll be able to take such a long leap," Hanuman said to the monkeys.

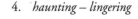

2. *hop – hop*   4. *haunting – lingering*
3. *shore – coast*

"Hanuman, you are the son of Vayu, the Wind God. You are the foremost among all of us who can leap but not as far as you can. Leap over the ocean. O swiftest one, how can you forget your heroic deeds which you performed when you were small?" Old Jambavana reminded Hanuman of his childhood when he had swallowed the Sun.

Mighty Hanuman began to increase in size. Waving his tail with joy, he attained his full strength. Then Hanuman closed his eyes and thought of Lord Rama. With his clear image in his heart, he leapt forward. There was not a moment's hesitation in his movements as he flew upwards into the clear sky. The entire monkey army watched the *splendour*[5] of Hanuman's *magnificent*[6] deed. It was a wonderful sight.

5. *splendour – glorious*   6. *magnificent – wonderful*

An Understanding

Q & A

Q. How many generals of his army did Sugriva call?

Ans. _____

_____

Q. To which direction did Hanuman take his army?

Ans. _____

_____

Q. What did Rama give to Hanuman and why?

Ans. _____

_____

Q. Who was Sampati?

Ans. _____

_____

Q. What did Jambavana remind Hanuman about and why?

_____

_____

Life-sketch

Prepare a life-sketch of any one of the following:

➤ Hanuman

➤ Angada

➤ Jambavana

➤ Sampati

Food for Thought

Sampati had burnt his wings long ago when he saved his brother Jatayu from a fire. He was blessed by the gods and given a boon. Find out about that boon and when did that boon come true.

Life Skills

Find out the story of hanuman's childhood and his mighty deeds. You may watch the movie 'Bal hanuman' and write a report on it.

Sundar Kand

Fascinating Leap

Sundar Kand begins with Hanuma's preparations to cross the ocean in search of Sita. Mighty Hanuman's flight over the ocean is described in all its glory. Hanuman's encounters with Mainaka and Sursa form important phases of his flight.

Then he gets a distant view of Lanka and enters the city in the darkness of the night. After some search he finds Sita in Ashok Vatika. He hands over Rama's token ring to her. Later he destroys the Ashok Vatika and the *rakshasas* imprison Hanuman. He is then presented before Ravana.

Hanuman warns Ravana about the imminent war if Sita is not handed back to Rama. Ravana gets angry and orders to kill the monkey. Ravana's younger brother Vibhishana intervenes and reminds Ravana that Hanuman was an envoy and he could not be killed as per law.

So Ravana orders his men to burn Hanuman's tail. But Hanuman frees himself and sets Lanka on fire with his burning tail.

At the end of Sundar Kand, he returns to Rama and gives him the news of Sita.

It is believed that this Kand is called Sundar (beautiful) because of the description of the beautiful things that Hanuman sees in the magnificent Lanka.

Hanuman Reaches Lanka

anuman flew at great speed with his arms outstretched and his long tail floating behind him.

The Ocean God knew about the good cause for which Hanuman was going to Lanka. He wanted to help Hanuman who was doing a great service to Lord Rama. The Ocean God

called Mainaka, the hidden mountain under the surface of the sea and told him, "Mainaka, I want you to rise above the surface of the sea, so that Hanuman can rest there for a while before continuing his journey towards Lanka."

Mainaka readily agreed and rose from the ocean. Assuming that Hanuman will come and rest here and take some *refreshments*[1] Mainaka Mountain covered himself with trees *laden*[2] with fruits.

As Mainaka stood waiting for Hanuman to *descend*[3] and relax for a while, Hanuman saw the mountain and assumed that it was an *obstacle*[4] in his path. He thrust his chest forward and knocked the mountain over. Mainaka Mountain took form of a man and said, "I'm sorry, if I've come in your way. I did not want to stop you. I've risen to help you. The Ocean God asked me to rise and give you a moment's *respite*[5] before you continue your journey towards Lanka. Take rest on my peak. Eat the delicious fruits and then continue with your journey after you are refreshed."

"I'm so sorry to have hurt you. But I cannot stop. I'm in a hurry. Still I thank you for your concern." Hanuman said to Mainaka as he rushed past him. Little did he know that another obstacle in the form of Sursa awaited him ahead.

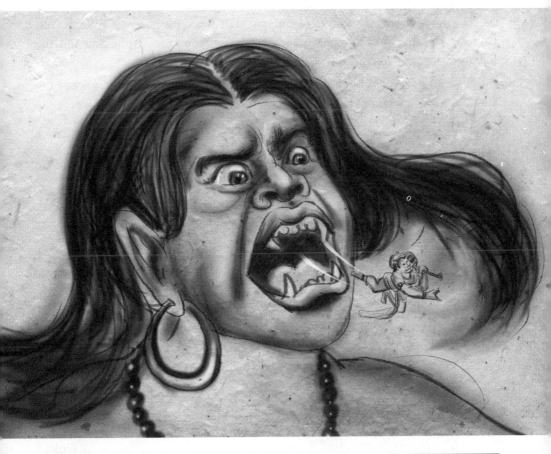

1. *refreshments – food and drink*
2. *laden – loaded*
3. *descend – go down*
4. *obstacle – barrier*
5. *respite – rest*

Sursa was the mother of serpents. She took the form of a *hideous*[6] demon and rose from the depths of the ocean.

She stopped Hanuman and said, "I am blessed with a boon that no one can get past me till I allow them. So you better enter my mouth first and then go on, if you can."

Seeing no way out, Hanuman *expanded*[7] himself. Sursa too went on expanding herself larger than Hanuman. Hanuman expanded further. This went on for some time till Hanuman had reached the size of a hundred *yojans*. Sursa looked equally big. Hanuman peeped into Sursa's open mouth. It was like a *fiery*[8] hell.

Suddenly Hanuman contracted his body to the size of a thumb and flew right into Sursa's opened mouth swiftly. With equal swiftness, he flew out of the mouth in an instant and said, "I've entered your mouth and fulfilled your boon. Now let me pass."

"That was clever," she said to Hanuman, "I'm Sursa, the queen of serpents. You have my blessings now. Go ahead and accomplish your goal. Unite Sita and the mighty Rama."

With all *hurdles*[9] behind him, Hanuman flew on happily. But this was not the end to the obstacles in his path.

---

6. *hideous – ugly*
7. *expanded – stretched*

8. *fiery – flaming*
9. *hurdles – barriers*

An Understanding

Q & A

Q. Who was Mainaka?

Ans. _____

_____

Q. Who sent Mainaka to Hanuman and why?

Ans. _____

_____

Q. Who was Sursa?

Ans. _____

_____

Q. How did Sursa try to stall Hanuman from going further?

_____

_____

Q. What did Hanuman do to fulfil Sursa's condition?

_____

_____

Comprehension

Read the passage given below and answer the questions that follow

"Once all mountains had wings and they could fly. Gods, sages, and other creatures were terrified that the mountains would fall on them anytime. So Indra started clipping wings of all the mountains with his thunderbolt. Luckily I was hurled away and thrown into the ocean with my wings intact. That was your father Vayu who saved me and helped me hide in this ocean. The Ocean God very kindly consented to accommodate me here. Today I've risen to return them a favour." Mainaka Mountain told Hanuman while he was on his way to Lanka.

1. Who used to have wings earlier?

_____

_____

2. Why were gods, sages, and other creatures scared?

_____

_____

3. What did Indra do to help the gods and sages?

_____

_____

4. Who was hurled and thrown into the ocean?

_____

_____

5. Who helped Mainaka Mountain?

_____

_____

6. How did Mainaka Mountain return the favour of Ocean God?

_____

_____

Food for Thought

Hanuman's tryst with Sursa shows that he was not just mighty but intelligent too. Explain how?

Life Skills

Arrange a trip to a coastal city and visit the beach. Take a look at the ocean and observe its vastness. Can you see anything beyond the ocean? Write a short note on your observation describing your feelings about the mighty ocean.

Ashok Vatika

Sun was like a pink ball of fire. Clouds rushed past Hanuman and the winds carried him over the ocean. Suddenly as Hanuman looked down there were no more rolling waves. There stood the green island of Lanka.

"I shall arouse everyone's curiosity if I enter Lanka in this immense form," Hanuman thought and quickly contracted his huge body to *revert*[1] it to its natural shape.

1. *revert – slip back*

Lanka looked beautiful like Amravati, the city of gods. Lanka was a vast place. It was situated on the top of a mountain. With its *dazzling*[2] golden buildings, it looked like a golden city hanging in the air. Lanka had been created by Vishwakarma, the architect of gods. Lanka once belonged to Kuber.

There was greenery all over the place. The trees were laden with delicious fruits and beautiful flowers. Birds nested on their *swaying*[3] tops. The lakes were filled with beautiful lotuses.

"How will I find Sita in this huge place? Sampati said he saw her sitting in a garden. But which garden…this place is full of gardens," thought Hanuman. He wanted to meet Sita alone so that he could give her Rama's ring.

So he thought of a plan. He decided to make himself smaller and sneak into the king's palace. Hanuman hid behind a tree and waited for the evening to fall.

The city of Lanka was lit with lamps. Lanka's beauty dazzled Hanuman. The mansions studded with gems, the roads made of gold, glittered in the golden light. He jumped over the walls and entered the palace without much difficulty. Hiding behind a bush he looked around carefully. He saw many charming women sleeping blissfully inside the palace but Sita could not be seen. They were all wearing glittering ornaments and looked quite content. Hanuman reasoned that none of them could be Sita because she would never adorn herself in those *shimmering*[4] jewels after separation from Rama nor would she look so content.

"I do not know what she looks like. But my heart will know when I see her," thought Hanuman.

Even after a long search in and around the palace, Hanuman could not find Sita anywhere. Still he did not give up hope. He kept peeping into the rooms. It was while he was passing through one such room that he happened to look out of a small window. There was a lovely garden, gleaming in the shining moonlight.

Hanuman was small so he quickly stepped through that window and entered that garden. Huge flowers bloomed everywhere and their sweet fragrance filled the air.

Hanuman had reached Ashok Vatika.

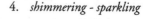

2. *dazzling – stunning*
3. *swaying – credible*

4. *shimmering - sparkling*

An Understanding

Q & A

Q. Why did Hanuman contract his huge form?

Ans. _____

_____

Q. Who created Lanka?

Ans. _____

_____

Q. Why did Hanuman wait for the evening to fall?

Ans. _____

_____

Q. Why was Hanuman sure that Sita would not be wearing glittering jewels?

Ans. _____

_____

Q. Where did Hanuman reach searching for Sita?

Ans. _____

_____

Make Sentence

Pick out the adjectives from these sentences and write a sentence with them

1. The trees were laden with delicious fruits and beautiful flowers.

   _____

   _____

2. The lakes were filled with beautiful lotuses.

   _____

   _____

3. It was difficult to find Sita in that huge palace.

   _____

   _____

4. The dazzling mansions and golden roads were attractive.

   _____

   _____

127

5. They were all wearing glittering ornaments.

   _____

   _____

6. Sita would never adorn herself in those shimmering jewels.

   _____

   _____

7. There was a lovely garden, gleaming in the shining moonlight.

   _____

   _____

8. Pretty flowers bloomed everywhere and their sweet fragrance filled the air.

   _____

   _____

Food for Thought

Describe the beauty of the city of Lanka in your
own words.

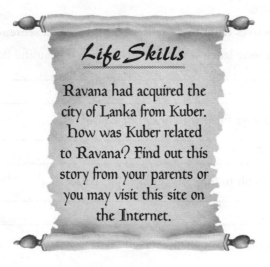

Life Skills

Ravana had acquired the
city of Lanka from Kuber.
how was Kuber related
to Ravana? Find out this
story from your parents or
you may visit this site on
the Internet.

19

Hanuman Meets Sita

Hanuman looked around in awe. There was something different about this place. It was quiet, pure, and serene. He was surprised to see such a place in Ravana's Lanka. Hanuman looked around in wonder.

Then he saw Sita. She was sitting on a pavilion. White as marble, the pavilion had a thousand pillars of beaten gold and steps of coral. She was sitting there silently surrounded with *rakshasis*. Her sad face was pale and *gaunt*[1]. The bright moonlight

1. *gaunt – lean*

made her look as pure as the white lily. Even though she looked sad and very thin from fasting, her face shone like moonbeam from the purity of her conduct. She was devoid of any glittering jewellery which other *rakshasis* were wearing.

As quietly as he could, Hanuman *swung*[2] through the trees till he reached behind the tree under which Sita was sitting. Suddenly Sita looked up.

Her eyes were filled with tears and heart with grief. In the past four months that she had spent in Ashok Vatika, not a single moment passed when she did not think about her past life.

With a *sigh*[3], she closed her eyes. Two drops of tears fell from her eyes. She could hear Ravana's voice *thundering*[4] in her ears, "Marry me. I will make you my queen. My Lanka is full of jewels and gold and other treasures. They will all be yours." But Sita never gave him any response.

---

2. *swung - swayed*
3. *sigh - exhale noisily*

4. *thundering – roaring*

Hanuman waited till all the *rakshasis* lay snoring. He sat quietly hidden under the trees watching Sita who was the *epitome*[5] of purity. When all the *rakshasis* dozed off, Hanuman hopped on to a branch right above Sita and began chanting Rama's name in a soft voice. He was careful not to wake the *rakshasis*.

"A noble prince named Rama lived in Ayodhya. He was the son of King Dasharatha. He was the greatest human to walk on earth. One day…"

In this way Hanuman began narrating Rama's story from Rama's childhood to his marriage, exile, kidnapping of Sita, and the alliance with Sugriva.

Sita could not believe her ears. Hanuman's words fell on her ears like the sweetest *melody*[6] on earth.

"Who are you? How do you know so much about my Lord Rama?" Sita asked him.

Just then, tiny Hanuman jumped before Sita and folded his hands as he spoke softly, "I'm Hanuman, humble servant of your Lord. I have been sent by Rama to enquire about your welfare. "

Sita nodded her head and said, "But how can I be sure that you are not one of Ravana's men in disguise. *Convince*[7] me that my Lord Rama has sent you?"

Hanuman took out a ring and placed it in Sita's palm. "I'm sure you recognise this ring. It has been given by Lord Rama to me to give it to you so that you would be convinced that I am sent by him."

Sita's eyes filled with tears of joy. She recognised her husband's ring. She cried, "O dear monkey, please tell me how is my lord? Does he remember me? When is he coming to take me back?" With each word tears spilled out of her eyes.

Hanuman could not bear to see Sita cry.

"Do not cry. Lord Rama will rescue you from this hell. I just came here to make sure you are here. Rama is waiting on the other shore of the ocean with a huge army of monkeys and bears. As soon as I go back and give him the news, he will attack Lanka and kill that *wretched*[8] Ravana."

Hanuman folded his hands and continued, "Now I must go back and give your news to Rama. But you don't worry. We shall be back soon in full strength."

"Wait," Sita took out a pin from her hair and handed it to Hanuman. Rama had carved out this pin for her from a branch during their stay at Chitrakoot. "Give this

---

5. *epitome – personification*
6. *melody – song*

7. *convince – prove to*
8. *wretched – pitiful*

to my lord. I have nothing else to give him. Please tell him that Sita is waiting for him with bated breath."

Before leaving, Hanuman decided to destroy the Ashok Vatika. This garden was Ravana's favourite. If anyone spoiled his garden, his *wrath*[9] would consume all of them. Hanuman took a flying leap and landed on a diamond-studded tree nearby. He started breaking its golden branches. Then he stomped his feet on the crystal pond and broke its letting all its water run out. He crushed the jewelled fish. The *rakshasas* on guard heard the commotion and surrounded him.

---

9.   *wrath – anger*

An Understanding

Q & A

Q. Where was Sita sitting in the Ashok Vatika?

Ans. _____

_____

Q. What had Ravana said to Sita?

Ans. _____

_____

Q. How did Hanuman introduce himself to Sita?

Ans. _____

_____

Q. How did Hanuman convince Sita that he was sent by Rama?

Ans. _____

_____

Q. What gift did Sita give for Rama and why?

Ans. _____

_____

Comprehension

Write a paragraph on how Hanuman felt about Ashok Vatika and what was his first impression of Sita.

_____

_____

_____

_____

_____

_____

_____

Food for Thought

Describe Ashok Vatika in your own words.

Life Skills

Gardens have always attracted human beings because of their beauty and serenity. Go to a nearby garden in the morning and enjoy the freshness in it. You may even visit the Mughal Gardens in Delhi which open during spring season.

20

Lanka Dahan

Ravana's guards tried to catch Hanuman but he was too quick for all of them. As the guards came near him, he made himself so small that they could not see him and Hanuman slipped between their legs. While they were looking for Hanuman on the ground, Hanuman made himself so big that he towered over them. In this way, he made them *chase*[1] him all over the place.

When the guards failed to capture Hanuman, Ravana ordered his son Indrajit to

---

1. *chase – pursue*

catch the naughty monkey. Indrajit released Brahma's weapon, *Brahmastra*, on Hanuman. This weapon could never miss its target so Hanuman got trapped and fell down on the ground. Hanuman was brought to Ravana's court.

"Who are you?" Ravana thundered.

"I'm Hanuman, servant of Lord Rama," Hanuman said proudly, holding his head high. "Let Sita go and ask for the forgiveness from Rama. Otherwise, I assure you that death has come to you in the form of Sita. Rama is the greatest warrior on earth and today he has entire monkey army of Sugriva with him. If you do not come to your senses now, your golden Lanka will be consumed by Sita's *effulgence*[2] and the fire of Rama's wrath. The entire army of monkeys and bears is waiting on the shore. They will be here in a matter of days to destroy you and take Sita back."

Ravana was *incensed*[3] at the *audacity*[4] of that monkey whom he felt like crushing under his feet. "I'll kill you here and now," he shouted.

---

2. *effulgence – brilliance*
3. *incensed – angry*

4. *audacity – courage*

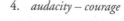

Just then, Ravana's younger brother, Vibhishana, got up and said, "O King, do not forget he is a messenger. The law *prohibits*[5] the king to kill an envoy. It is not fit for you to *stoop*[6] so low."

To this Ravana said, "Law forbids killing an envoy. But we can punish him in some other way. A monkey closely guards his tail. Set his tail on fire and release him. This way we will not have killed him, but he'll die all the same."

The *rakshasas* caught Hanuman who was still tied in the ropes and dragged him out of the courtroom. Grabbing his tail, they wrapped it in a cloth. Hanuman kept *elongating*[7] his tail and the *rakshasas* kept wrapping it with more and more clothes. Tired of the endless exercise, they finally dipped it in oil and set it on fire.

Hanuman leapt forward with a *deafening*[8] roar and jumped high into the air. He grew his body to an enormous size so that the ropes binding him snapped like weak threads. His burning tail was as long as a python.

5. *prohibits – forbids*
6. *stoop – bend*

7. *elongating – lengthen*
8. *deafening – loud*

With his tail blazing, Hanuman ran along the roofs of Lanka and set all the houses on fire. Trees, houses, chariots, granary – all went up in flames. People started running *hither tither*[9].

Hanuman burnt the entire Lanka but he did not touch the Ashok Vatika. Before taking the leap, he turned around to take one last look at the golden city of Lanka. It had now turned black. Hanuman smiled, satisfied at his handiwork and turned towards the sea.

---

9. *hither tither – here and there*

An Understanding

Q & A

Q. How did Hanuman escape Ravana's guards?

Ans. _____

_____

Q. Who caught Hanuman and how?

Ans. _____

_____

Q. Who stopped Ravana from killing Hanuman and how?

Ans. _____

_____

Q. What was the alternate way chosen by Ravana to kill Hanuman?

Ans. _____

_____

Q. What did Hanuman do after his tail was set on fire?

Ans. _____

_____

Fill in the blanks

1. Hanuman was caught by Indrajit using ………….

2. Indrajit displayed………to his father like a big achievement.

3. Vibhishana was Ravana's…………..

4. The *rakshasas* wrapped Hanuman's……………in cloth.

5. Hanuman burnt the entire………..

Food for Thought

Why did hanuman burn the whole Lanka but spare
Ashok Vatika ?

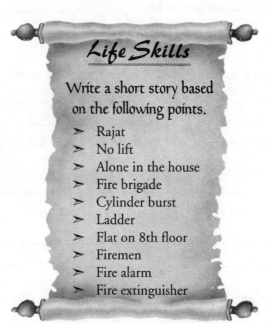

Life Skills

Write a short story based
on the following points.

➤ Rajat
➤ No lift
➤ Alone in the house
➤ Fire brigade
➤ Cylinder burst
➤ Ladder
➤ Flat on 8th floor
➤ Firemen
➤ Fire alarm
➤ Fire extinguisher

Yuddha Kand

Devastating War

Rama appreciates Hanuman and welcomes him after he returns from Lanka. He embraces him after hearing his brave deeds.

Rama is glad that Hanuman has done something worthy of a noble servent. Then Rama reflects upon the problem of how to cross the ocean.

Rama builds a bridge across the ocean and reaches Lanka with a large army of monkeys and bears. Vibhishana, Ravana's brother, joins them in the war leaving his brother whom he feels does not adhere the path of *dharma*.

The great war ensues.

One by one, all the *rakshasas* are killed. Ravana's entire family including Kumbhakarna and Indrajit are also killed and finally Ravana is slain too.

Sita is rescued by Ram and Vibhishana is crowned the king of Lanka.

Everything goes well but Rama has a doubt in his mind. So after the great victory, Rama takes Sita's *Agni Pariksha* before returning to Ayodhya.

Rama, Lakshmana, and Sita return to Ayodhya where Rama is crowned the King of Kosala amidst fanfare.

Crossing the Ocean

Hanuman bowed before Rama and told him all that had happened in Lanka. He told him that Sita was a prisoner but she was unharmed.

"I met her. She is well, but is a prisoner in Ravana's palace garden, Ashok Vatika. She only thinks of you and has been *fasting*[1]. She asked me to give you this." Hanuman took out Sita's hair pin and handed it over to Rama.

As Rama took Sita's pin in his hand, his heart filled with sorrow. Controlling his

---

1. *fasting – not eating anything*

 # The Grand Finale

24

*J*ndrajit sat before the deity in his family temple trying to complete a special sacrifice. If he was able to complete this sacrifice he would be bestowed with special powers following which no God or human will ever be able to defeat him. Indrajit already had many powerful weapons in his possession. He could hide behind the clouds, he could change his form, he could move with incredible speed. He had achieved all these powers through *penance*[1] and special sacrifices from time to time.

Vibhishana knew that Indrajit would be performing the sacrifice at the temple as it was his practice before each war.

"Come I'll take you to the place where he is performing the sacrifice. Kill him then and there before he manages to complete his special sacrifice because after that he will be *invincible*[2]," Vibhishana told Lakshmana.

Lakshmana set out quickly. He was ready to take revenge from him for hurting him so badly and giving so much grief to his brother Rama.

Lakshmana sent a shower of arrows upon Indrajit. His spell broken, Indrajit opened his eyes. Seeing Lakshmana, he turned towards him with a *sneer*[3] and attacked back with a *vengeance*[4].

Indrajit fought back. Showing no signs of *fatigue*[5], the two warriors kept on fighting with each other.

Finally Lakshmana took out his most powerful arrow, *Indrastra*, and hurled it at Indrajit. *Indrastra* never missed its target. Flying though the air like a streak of lightning, the *Indrastra* severed Indrajit's head off. His crown fell to the ground and golden earrings flung far off.

Ravana was crying bitterly. His pride and delight, his dearest son Indrajit was no more. His *lust*[6] had consumed all his sons. Indrajit had once overcome Indra, the

---

1. *penance – reparation*
2. *invincible – unbeatable*
3. *sneer – scorn*
4. *vengeance – retaliation*
5. *fatigue – exhaustion*
6. *lust – desire*

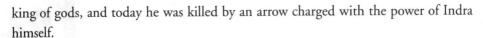

king of gods, and today he was killed by an arrow charged with the power of Indra himself.

He vowed to take revenge from Rama for the deaths of Kumbhakarna and Indrajit.

He ordered his charioteer to get his divine chariot ready. His chariot had a golden banner and had gems fitted all around it. It was driven by eight swift strong black horses. The chariot was equipped with all the latest weapons. The moment his chariot landed at his door, Ravana leapt into it with the swiftness of a tiger. He asked his charioteer to get down and took over the reins himself. Ravana chose to take the fifth gate, the gate of illusion, and rose up like a black swan into the sky.

The morning sun hid behind the cloud of darkness as the sky darkened when Ravana's chariot entered the battlefield. Following him was a small army of the demons riding on horses, elephants, and chariots. They were the last of the warriors left in Lanka.

The fierce battle began.

Ravana drove straight to the spot where Rama stood with Hanuman and Lakshmana.

Rama sent a volley of arrows at Ravana as he approached. The arrows hit him on several of his heads. Blood spurted out but Ravana kept on laughing like a maniac and moving ahead on his chariot. Rama sent some powerful arrows slicing off some of Ravana's many heads. But they grew back at once.

"Rama was born for this moment *precisely*[7]," someone whispered from the heaven above.

Rama said a prayer, invoked a *mantra* and sent the *Rudrastra* to pierce Ravana's golden armour.

Ravana managed to *dodge*[8] the arrow and hurled back *Asurastra* to Rama. It turned into wild beasts that roared and attacked Rama.

---

7. *precisely – accurately*   8. *dodge – avoid*

But Rama retaliated with the *Agneyastra* which burnt all the beasts to *cinders*[9].

Ravana shot the serpent arrows but Rama killed them with eagle arrows.

At last Ravana took out an enormous javelin in his hands which was smoking and hissing at its pointed tip. Ravana hurled it at Rama. Rama countered the javelin with a shower of arrows which should have burnt down the weapon but the arrows fell down from the fury of the javelin and were burnt to ashes.

Rama immediately took out the *Shakti* weapon which Indra had given him and hurled it in the air with all his force. The javelin and the *Shakti collided*[10] mid-air. The javelin broke into a thousand pieces and fell on the ground. It was not hissing anymore. Its powers were exhausted.

Time passed as the hours flew by. Sugriva, Hanuman, Angad, Jamabavan, and Vibhishana watched the fierce battle with open mouths. Ravana seemed invincible and that is what was worrying all of them. No one except Vibhishana knew the secret of Ravana's death. He knew Ravana had the *potion*[11] of immortality (*amrit*) in his navel. Vibhishana went to Rama and whispered this secret into his ear. He urged Rama to aim his arrow at his navel.

"Use Brahma's weapon *Brahmastra* against him. His moment of death has arrived," he prompted Rama.

Rama used *Brahmastra* given to him by Sage Agastya and sent it flying towards Ravana, aiming at his navel.

The arrow struck Ravana's navel directly at the spot where *amrit* lay, making him immortal. The *Brahmastra* sucked up all the *amrit* from his navel and took Ravana's life. Ravana's lifeless body plunged onto the earth.

Ravana's death was *proclaimed*[12] by the monkeys and everyone rejoiced at Rama's victory. The sky resounded with the beating of drums and loud chanting of 'Jai Shri Rama'.

News of Ravana's death spread like wildfire. Ravana's wife Mandodari ran out of the palace barefoot, her hair *disheveled*[13], her face wet with tears. She ran straight to the *gory*[14] battlefield and wept *piteously*[15].

Vibhishana cremated his brother Ravana as none of Ravana's sons had survived. After the funeral, Vibhishana took the *mandatory*[16] bath and came to meet Rama who

---

9. *cinders – ashes*
10. *collided – crashed*
11. *potion – brew*
12. *proclaimed – announced*

13. *disheveled – untidy*
14. *gory – horrific*
15. *piteously – pathetically*
16. *mandatory – customarym*

was sitting in a meeting with Lakshmana standing beside him. Sugriva, Hanuman, Jambavaa, and Angada were all present at the meeting.

As Vibhishana bowed before Rama, he nodded and said to all, "Vibhishana has been devoted and loyal to us. He is fit to be the king of Lanka. He is the rightful *claimant*[17] to the throne of Lanka as none of his elder brothers or Ravana's sons are alive. We must crown him as the king of Lanka without any further delay."

Everyone cheered as Vibhishana was made the king of Lanka.

---

17. *claimant – applicant*

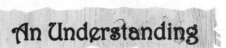

An Understanding

Q & A

Q. Why was Indrajit sitting in front of the deity?

Ans. _____

_____

Q. Who killed Indrajit and how?

Ans. _____

_____

Q. Why could Rama not kill Ravana?

Ans. _____

_____

Q. Why did Rama shoot Ravana in his navel?

Ans. _____

_____

Q. Who became the king of Lanka after the demise of Ravana?

Ans. _____

_____

Choose the right form of verb

Fill in the right form of the verb given in the bracket in these sentences. Also make a new sentence with another form of the same verb.

1. Rama's arrow ....Ravana on several of his heads. (hit)

_____

_____

2. Agneyastra ....all the beasts to cinders. (burn)

_____

_____

3. Rama ....a prayer with his bow in hand. (say)

_____

_____

4. Mandodari...............piteously on Ravana's demise. (weep)

_____

_____

5. After the funeral, Vibhishana ....the mandatory bath. (take)

_____

_____

Food for thought

Imagine the plight of Mandodari who had been warning Ravana again and again to return Sita. Write a short paragraph as Mandodari who laments on the death of her husband Ravana.

Life Skills

Defection is a common practice. Manyatimes people have left their kings or brothers or fathers to join hands with the enemy camp. This makes one vulnerable as their secrets are known to the defector and it becomes an advantage to the enemy with whom the defector joins hands. Search the history of India and world history and write about five such defectors who shook hands with the enemies.

25

Sita's Agni Pariksha

With everything settled in Lanka, it was time for Rama and Lakshmana to retreat with their army.

Rama turned to mighty Hanuman and said, "Take king Vibhishana's permission and go to Ashok Vatika. Tell Sita that Lakshmana, Sugriva, and I are waiting here for her eagerly. Also tell her about my victory and Ravana's demise. Then bring her here with all due respect."

Sita was surprised that Rama had not come himself, nor did he send Lakshmana to bring her to him. However, she kept quiet and sat in the palanquin sent by Vibhishana to take her to Rama.

Her eyes filled with eternal love and *compassion*[1] for Rama when she saw him after such a long time.

Sita *alighted*[2] from the palanquin and came near Rama hoping to hear her name from his lips. She stood there with her eyes downcast with shyness and her heart full of love for her husband who managed to free her out of his love for her. She waited….and waited… and waited for a long time which seemed like *eternity*[3]. When she did not hear a word from Rama, she looked at him. She was surprised to see her husband's back towards her. He had turned his face away.

"My lord, why are looking away from me? Talk to me," Sita urged.

Rama's face darkened. He spoke harshly to Sita, "I've won this war, *vanquished*[4] the enemy and rescued you from him. But don't mistake this victory as your own. I did not fight this battle just for your sake. I waged this war to fight against the evil. I fought this war to free this earth from an evil demon who had become a burden on the face of this earth. Now that the war is over, you may live wherever you wish to. You have lived in another man's house for so long that it gives me no joy to get you back unless you prove your purity to me by passing through a fiery ordeal. Unless proved thus, I cannot take you back."

Sita was *stunned*[5]. He did not trust her!

---

1. *compassion – kindness*
2. *alighted – got down*
3. *eternity – time without end*

4. *vanquished – defeated*
5. *stunned – shocked*

Not in her wildest dreams had she ever imagined that her husband, the centre of her life and soul, could ever utter such words. Tired and weak from months of fasting, Sita held on to the tree nearby.

Lakshmana looked over at Rama with pain in his eyes. He could not see Sita, the one whom he revered most after his mother; suffer such humility in front of the entire army and people of Lanka.

As he was about to protest loudly, Sita stopped him by raising her hands. Her eyes held a fiery look now. Though tears were trying to come to the fore, she fought to keep them back. Lifting her head proudly, Sita said in a soft voice, "My lord, my life and my soul – all belong to you. Never in my life have I ever thought of another man. Yet you, my lord, break my heart with those cruel words which are sharper than your arrows. But I'll *abide*⁶ by your command because that is the *dharma* of a woman."

There was a hushed silence all around them. Rama's voice broke the silence, "If

6. *abide – bear*

you are as pure as you say then you should not have any objection to test yourself in the sacred fire. Lakshmana will build a fire for you. You walk through that fire. If you come out unharmed, it means that Lord Agni himself proves your purity. I'll then have no objection to take you back as my wife."

While Lakshmana got ready to prepare the pyre, Sita lifted her head proudly and said to Rama, "Test me, will you! Very well, then. Have it your way. But I wish to Agni to consume me after proclaiming my purity. I do not wish to live a day longer after facing such shame."

With tears falling down his cheeks, Lakshmana built the pyre silently and lit the fire.

The audience gasped in horror as Sita stepped into the raging fire and sat down at the very centre. "O God of fire, you know I'm pure. If my heart has never strayed from Rama, then please protect me till I've proved my innocence. After that give me solace in your loving flames forever."

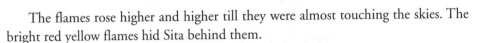

The flames rose higher and higher till they were almost touching the skies. The bright red yellow flames hid Sita behind them.

Suddenly, there was a flash of lightning. Agni, the Fire God appeared within flames and said to Rama, "Sita is as pure as the *panchtatvas*[7] in this universe. Take her back and treasure her." Saying so, he lifted her in his arms and brought her by Rama's side.

Sita looked beautiful with a mighty glow on her face. The golden ornaments sparkled on her arms, ears, and around her neck. She looked like the morning sun – pure and beautiful.

Rama said to the gods, "Sita had to go through this test to prove to the world that I, the son of Dasharatha, was not blinded by his love for a woman. I wanted everyone in this world to believe in Sita for her purity and not just because she is my wife. She is protected by the power of her own *chastity*[8]."

Saying this Rama stepped forward and took Sita's hand. He smiled lovingly into her eyes and spoke softly into her ear, "From the very beginning I knew you were pure as the holy Ganges. But how would others know this until you prove it to them. Today you have shown to the world the power of chastity and purity. You are my beloved and not for a single moment I doubted your innocence. I simply had to do this to show the world how pure you are. I hope you understand this and forgive me."

Sita smiled weakly. A light shower from heavens blessed Rama and Sita.

---

7. *panchtatvas – Five elements of nature*   8. *chastity – purity*

An Understanding

Q & A

Q. Whom did Rama send to bring Sita?

Ans. _____

_____

Q. Why was Sita surprised when she saw her husband's back towards her?

Ans. _____

_____

Q. What did Rama want from Sita?

Ans. _____

_____

Q. Who built the pyre?

Ans. _____

_____

Q. Who announced to the world that Sita was pure?

Ans. _____

_____

Comprehension

Write a dialogue between Rama and Lakshmana as Lakshmana tries to convince his brother to be fair to Sita.

_____

_____

_____

_____

_____

_____

_____

Food for Thought

Do you agree with the argument Rama gave in favour of
Sita's *Agni Pariksha*? Give reasons for your answer.

Life Skills

Sita's *Agni Pariksha* depicts
that women and fire have a
strange combine. Our society
has many such other cases
where women are tested with
fire. *Sati* and *Johar* are two
such social evils which have
fire and women at their helm.
Find out more about the
social evils *Sati* and *Johar*
and write a report on them.

Uttara Rand

Post Script

*R*ama and Sita return to their royal life in Ayodhya. They live many years till Rama learns about the discontent among his people because he had accepted Sita who had lived in another man's house for so many months.

Rama being the loyal and just king banishes Sita to the forest.

Sage Valmiki looks after Sita in the forest. He takes her to his hermitage where she gives birth to her twin sons – Luva and Kusha.

When the twins grow up Sage Valmiki trains them in the art of warfare and statesmanship in the same manner as a prince would be taught.

Rama performs *Ashvamedha Yagya* in which the twins fight with Rama's army and defeats them all. When Rama learns that they are his children, he rejoices.

He meets Sita but refuses to accept her as his wife because of the fear of discontentment in Ayodhya. Sita, feeling humiliated, hails Mother Earth to accept her. Mother Earth takes in Sita and she is separated from her beloved husband Rama forever.

Rama is broken hearted and returns to Ayodhya with his sons. Soon he too departs to heaven to meet Sita.

26

Rama – the King of Ayodhya

*R*ama along with Lakshmana and Sita climbed on to the chariot of flowers and headed towards Ayodhya. As soon as their chariot reached Ayodhya, Bharata rushed to touch Rama's feet, who stopped him midway and embraced him.

He took Rama, Lakshmana, and Sita inside the palace where the three queens were waiting for them *eagerly*[1].

Soon Rama was crowned the king of Ayodhya. Lakshmana stood beside him and Bharata sat at his brother's feet while Shatrughana held the royal umbrella over his head.

After a fourteen-year-long *amavasya*[2], today on the advent of *amavasya*, Ayodhya rejoiced by lighting the lamps all around. This *amavasya* brought light through rows of lamps, bringing in *deepavali* in the lives of the people of Ayodhya.

Ayodhya prospered in the years that followed. Rama ruled with Sita by his side. People of Ayodhya were healthy and happy. Rain gods were pleased with them. Rains came on time and the bumper crops followed year after year. People shared their wealth among each other. There was no place for greed, jealousy, or hatred in their hearts. There was no discrimination of rich and poor. There were no thieves or beggars in Ayodhya. The trade flourished and the country grew wealthier by the day.

Rama was a just, brave, and handsome king. The laws were fair and equal for all. People never locked their houses even if they ventured out for long periods. His rule came to be known as *Rama-Rajya*.

The weather was always wonderful. The summers were *mild*[3], the winters were warm, and the autumn never seemed to touch Ayodhya. It was spring time throughout the year. The sun shone brightly in the sky. The sky was blue and the wind blew softly. The flowers bloomed in large numbers in the fresh breeze and their fragrance filled the atmosphere. It was nature's *bounty*[4] which made the people of Ayodhya sing when they worked in the fields. They returned home to their loving families. Smiles and laughter was spread all around.

Even the gods looked down and compared the heaven with the beauty of the city of Ayodhya.

Hanuman stayed on in Ayodhya while the other monkeys of Sugriva's army left Ayodhya soon after Rama's coronation. Hanuman decided to spend his entire life at the feet of Rama.

When Sugriva came to know of Hanuman's decision of staying back, he felt bad. He *chided*[5] Hanuman for switching loyalties. But Hanuman, though aggrieved at Sugriva's words, remained *nonchalant*[6].

---

1. *eagerly – impatiently*
2. *amavasya – no-moon night*
3. *mild – gentle*
4. *bounty – reward*
5. *chided – reproached*
6. *nonchalant – indifferent*

"Show me proof of your love and devotion to Rama," Sugriva had questioned Hanuman in Rama's court before leaving for Kishkindha.

Hanuman merely smiled and while chanting Rama's name, he tore off his chest with his own hands.

Everyone in the court, including Sugriva, was surprised to see Rama and Sita seated on a throne in Hanuman's heart. Sugriva immediately freed Hanuman from all *bonds*[7] of monkey clan. He permitted him to stay with Rama forever.

Thus Hanuman stayed on.

7. *bonds – attachments*

An Understanding

Q & A

Q. In which chariot did Rama come back to Ayodhya?

Ans. _____

_____

Q. Who was crowned the King of Ayodhya?

Ans. _____

_____

Q. Why did Hanuman want to stay with Rama?

Ans. _____

_____

Q. What did Sugriva ask Hanuman?

Ans. _____

_____

Q. Why did Sugriva free Hanuman from all bonds of the monkey clan?

Ans. _____

_____

Choose the correct option

1. Rama came back to Ayodhya with

   a. Sita ☐

   b. Lakshmana ☐

   c. Hanuman ☐

   d. All of them ☐

2. Rama was crowned the King of

   a. Lanka ☐

   b. Ayodhya ☐

   c. Mithila ☐

   d. Delhi ☐

3. Hanuman decided to spend his entire life at the feet of
    a. Lakshmana ☐
    b. Kaushalya ☐
    c. Shatrughana ☐
    d. Rama ☐

4. Sugriva freed Hanuman from all bonds of
    a. Human clan ☐
    b. Monkey clan ☐
    c. Bear clan ☐
    d. Elephant clan ☐

5. Rama's rule was called
    a. Rama-Rajya ☐
    b. Rama-Surya ☐
    c. Rajsuiya ☐
    d. Rama-Sita Rajya ☐

Food for Thought

Describe the rule of Rama and how different was it
from the rule of other kings?

Life Skills

'After a fourteen-year-
long amavasya, today on
the advent of amavasya,
Ayodhya rejoiced by lighting
the lamps all around.'
What does this signify
and how is it related to the
festival of Diwali that we
celebrate even today? Write
a small paragraph on it.

Sita's Banishment

It was a cool, refreshing morning in Ayodhya. Rama bid farewell to Sita as he headed towards the courtroom. When Rama entered the courtroom, he heard his ministers whispering amongst themselves. As soon as they saw him, they stopped *abruptly*[1].

Rama knew something was amiss because earlier also, he had noticed people *lurking*[2] in the corners of the palace and speaking in quiet voices.

In the evening, Rama called Bhadra, the chief of the spies.

"What's going on Bhadra? I know there is something wrong, but no one will speak to me about it. Now I order you to tell me what is it that everyone has been discussing secretly which I'm not aware of," Rama said.

Bhadra spoke hesitantly, "My lord, the people of Ayodhya speak highly of you. My lord, people say that you did a great job by killing the demon Ravana and rescuing Sita. But they do not feel that Sita is fit to be your queen after staying with Ravana for a long time."

Rama sat still in his chamber, deep in thought, trying to chart his course of action in such a situation. He had not imagined in the wildest of his dreams that such a *gossip*[3] was doing rounds in Ayodhya.

Rama was the king. He was the ideal of his subjects. He had to set the standards to be followed by others. Although he was the husband of Sita who was convinced of the purity and innocence of his wife, but Rama was a king first. As a king Rama had to be very careful in his conduct because he was a public figure and very open to criticism.

Rama stayed awake all night. It was a night of grief and anguish. His heart was heavy with pain for himself and Sita. The next day dawned and saw Rama in

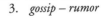

1. *abruptly – suddenly*
2. *lurking – hiding*

3. *gossip – rumor*

a *gloomy*[4] mood. In the evening, as Rama moved towards the palace garden to get some fresh air, one of his spies came to him and said, "Your majesty, pardon me. I've heard a washerman speak to his wife these words which I cannot even repeat in your presence. But I've been instructed by our chief Bhadra to report even the smallest details to you. He was *berating*[5] his wife. He questioned her absence in the night. He said that he was not a great person like Rama who embraced Sita even though she lived with Ravana for months. He refused to accept her and asked her to go away."

Rama stood still for a while, then dismissed the spy. He now knew he would have to abandon Sita on the *behest*[6] of the people of Ayodhya…to set an example for them. But, nevertheless, he would never have anyone else take her place.

4. *gloomy – sad*
5. *berating – rebuking*

6. *behest – command*

Then he called Lakshmana and ordered him, "Take Sita to the forest tomorrow morning and leave her just outside the borders of the kingdom. Sage Valmiki's hermitage lies on the banks of river Tamsa. Leave her there and come back quickly. She has been saying that she would like to visit the sages who live by the Ganga. Let her wishes be fulfilled."

Rama could sense Lakshmana start in horror. But he raised his hand to prevent him from protesting.

Neither did Rama explain the situation nor did Lakshmana ask him the reason, because both had sensed the *inevitable*[7] – they were about to lose that sweet loving human being who always stood by them in the times of need.

The next morning after getting the chariot ready, Lakshmana went inside the palace and touched Sita's feet, "The king has asked me to take you to the banks of the Ganga to the settlement of the sages there."

Sita was delighted.

On the way, Sita kept *pouring* her heart out to Lakshmana praising Rama and his just rule, but Lakshmana kept staring ahead. He drove the chariot with a straight face refusing to meet Sita's eyes till he *broke down*[8].

She asked him gently, "Why are you crying, Lakshmana. Is there something wrong?"

Lakshmana wiped his tears and said, "Rama has heard the harsh and unfair things people of Ayodhya keep saying about you in public. Even though you were declared innocent in my presence, Rama, the king of Ayodhya has denounced you to put a stop at the gossip and scandal that is doing rounds in Ayodhya. I have been asked to leave you here at Sage Valmiki's ashram. You are to live here from now on.'

Sita heard him quietly. Then she spoke in a voice so soft that it was hardly *audible*[9], "If that is my lord's wish then so be it. I shall live happily at the ashram."

She did not cry. Her lips *quivered*[10] but her eyes were dry. Her mind was numb but very angry.

Soon the chariot came to a *halt*[11]. Sage Valmiki was waiting for them at the ashram. He stepped forward to bless Sita, "I saw in my mind's eye that you would come to me today. I know who you are and why you are here. Do not worry, none of us will ever ask you any question. We know that you are innocent. This *serene*[12] place will bring you peace. We will look after you as well as we can."

---

7. *inevitable – expected*
8. *broke down – cry*
9. *audible – easy to hear*

10. *quivered – trembled*
11. *halt – stop*
12. *serene – calm*

He looked at Lakshmana, who was by now weeping *inconsolably*[13], and told him, "You may leave now."

Without speaking a word, Lakshmana bent down to touch Sita's feet and then got into the chariot without meeting Sita's eyes.

---

13. *inconsolably – mournfully*

An Understanding

Q & A

Q. Who was Bhadra?

Ans. _____

_____

Q. What did Bhadra tell Rama?

Ans. _____

_____

Q. What made Rama decide to banish Sita?

Ans. _____

_____

Q. Whom did Rama call to take Sita away?

Ans. _____

_____

Q. Where did Rama send Sita?

Ans. _____

_____

Fill in the blanks

1. When Rama entered the courtroom he heard his ministers............

2. Rama consulted ....often about the welfare of the people.

3. Being a ....Rama had to set ideals for his subjects.

4. Rama called ....and asked him to take Sita to the forest in the morning.

5. ....was waiting for Sita in his hermitage.

Food for Thought

Why could Lakshmana not retaliate against the injustice done to Sita by Rama? Give reasons for your answer.

Life Skills

Most of the hermitages were built on the river banks. What could be the reason behind it? On the Internet find out the whereabouts of the river Tamsa where Sage Valmiki's hermitage was situated.

Luva and Kusha

The days passed slowly for Sita in Valmiki's ashram. Sage Valmiki treated her like his own daughter but not like a queen. Though earlier Sita had lived in a forest for fourteen years, but now it was different. At that time, she was with her husband Rama and that made all the difference. Even without any jewels and fineries, she was the queen of her lord's heart. Now she felt *dejected*[1].

1. *dejected – crestfallen*

Sita learnt many things at the ashram, which she had not learnt earlier – not even during the exile days with her husband.

She learnt to milk cows, clean cowsheds, to clean the grains, grind the flour, to tend to tiny saplings in the ashram, and numerous other little chores which till now her maids used to do. Initially she cried in the quietness of her hut. Then she resigned to her fate. She became more spiritual and spent most of her time in the company of the sages in the ashram.

Seven months after Sita came into the hermitage, she gave birth to twin sons. When Valmiki got the news he immediately rushed to bless the boys. He chanted the holy *mantras* and took some grass in one hand. Then he spoke to the old woman attending to Sita, "The child, who was born first should be cleansed with this *kusha* grass purified by chants. He shall be named Kusha."

Then he picked up another handful of grass and chanted some more *mantras*. Handing over that grass to the other woman standing there, he said, "He, who was born next should be cleaned with this *luva* grass and he will be known as Luva."

In the night, Valmiki drew their horoscope and was surprised to find that their horoscope was of replica of their father, Lord Rama's horoscope. The horoscope revealed that the two boys would be victorious in battle and would grow up with virtues like modesty, courage, and accomplishments in every other skill.

As Sita lay beside her twin sons, she longed to let Rama know that their sons were born, but she had no way of informing him.

As a last ray of hope, she thought, "Maybe he will send for me soon or someone else to find out how I am, then I can inform him about the birth of his sons."

But none ever came from Ayodhya.

The great sage Valmiki nurtured them with tender care in the lap of nature. The two boys filled Sita's days with joy and laughter. She sang to them and told them stories. She did not miss her previous life so much now as she had her two little companions to make her days full and content.

The days turned into weeks and soon the months passed without Sita realising it. The sages told them stories, the women spoilt them with their love and younger

sages were their playmates.

Months turned into years and the boys grew up into fine lads. Both the brothers were well-behaved. They showed utmost respect for their mother Sita and guru Valmiki.

Sage Valmiki began their training in the same way as a *kshatriya*[2] should be brought up. He taught them the skill of archery and all the *scriptures*[3] which once their father had also studied. He also taught them how to perform their religious and royal duties.

Valmiki was careful in their education because he knew that one day these twins would be required to undertake great activities in war and statesmanship. He knew that these twins would grow up to be the kings of Ayodhya. So he imparted training fit for a king. Besides the usual education, Valmiki taught them the Ramayana which he had himself composed. Luva and Kusha learnt and recited the epic. Valmiki also taught them to play musical instruments while singing the Ramayana. When the boys sang Ramayana in their sweet voice, the music sounded divine.

The twins were taught everything under the sun except for one thing – that they were the sons of the great king Rama whose *saga*[4] they sang in the form of Ramayana and the queen in the story of Rama was none other than their own mother.

---

2. *kshatriya – warrior caste*
3. *scriptures – holy books*

4. *saga – tale*

An Understanding

Q & A

Q. How was Sita treated in the ashram?

Ans. _____

_____

Q. What were the things that Sita learnt in Sage Valmiki's ashram?

Ans. _____

_____

Q. What were Sita's twin sons named and why?

Ans. _____

_____

Q. How did Sage Valmiki train them like *kshatriyas* and why?

Ans. _____

_____

Q. Which epic was learnt and sang by Luva and Kusha?

Ans. _____

_____

Fill in the blanks

Fill in the blanks by choosing the correct word from the box

1. Sage Valmiki treated Sita like his own ………..(son/daughter)

2. Sita spent most of her time in the company of the ……………(sages/cows)

3. The horoscope of both the boys were identical to that of their………(mother/father)

4. The two brothers learnt all the skills of a ……………..(brahmin/kshatriya)

5. Luva and Kusha sang the epic of Ramayana written by Sage………………(Vashishtha/Valmiki)

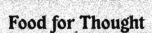

Food for Thought

Write a diary entry of a day in the life of Sita as she tries
to adjust to the ways of ashram initially.

Life Skills

horoscopes are a part of
astrology. Indian astrology
is based on stars and
constellations. Is astrology
a science
or not? Find out more
about this intriguing
subject.

The Ashwamedha Horse

*I*n the meanwhile, Rama ruled in Ayodhya all these years. He never tried to find out about Sita and her well-being.

One day Rama decided to perform *Ashvamedha Yagya*. He called his three brothers and instructed them to invite all the sages and brahmins to the *yagya*. With their blessings, Rama wanted to let loose the horse of the *yagya*.

All the preparations were done but there was one problem. No holy sacrifice, especially *yagya*, can be successful without the presence of husband and wife together. Rama had never remarried after *abandoning*[1] Sita. Since Sita was not there, Valmiki asked Rama to get a golden statue of Sita made and placed it to the left of Rama.

The *yagya* began with the holy chants of Vedic *mantras*. A white coloured horse stood nearby decorated beautifully with jewels and ornaments. Rama placed a *tilak* on the horse's forehead and released the horse.

In *Ashwamedha Yagya*, the horse moves throughout the territory and even beyond the area which is claimed by the king. Anyone who stops the horse has to wage a war against the king and if no one stops the horse then it is considered that the people of that area have accepted the *sovereignty*[2] of the king.

In the same vein, the horse of Rama's *Ashwamedha Yagya* moved on with Shatrughana and his army following him.

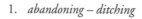

1. *abandoning – ditching*   2. *sovereignty – power*

It was a smooth sailing for them until the horse passed through the hermitage of Sage Valmiki.

It was a nice cool day. After finishing their lessons, Luva and Kusha were playing in the forest. Suddenly they saw a beautiful white horse charging towards them.

"What a lovely horse. Let us catch it. We shall take it to the ashram and keep it as a *pet*[3]." They ran after the horse and managed to catch it.

Suddenly there was a loud clatter of hooves and within seconds, a number of warriors surrounded the two boys. They were the soldiers from Rama's army who were following the horse to protect it.

The soldiers charged at the boys. But they had underestimated the two brothers. Luva and Kusha *retaliated*[4] with a mighty twang of their bow, the sound of which was deafening.

Rama's army ran back to their camp and told Shatrughana everything.

3. *pet – favourite animal*   4. *retaliate – strike back*

The huge army led by Shatrughana marched off to bring their *Ashvamedha* horse back.

The army swung into action but Luva and Kusha together were more than a match for all of them put together. The two young brothers proved to be better trained in the warfare than all the others put together. They did not miss their target even once.

Sage Valmiki had *envisaged*[5] all these events before they actually happened. He had prepared Luva and Kusha for such eventualities well. Today they had proved themselves to be worthy disciples of Valmiki.

People of Ayodhya had to be taught a lesson. Pride always has a fall, sooner or later. Ravana, too, paid for his pride. Ayodhya had shown its *haughtiness*[6] in abandoning their queen. Now the time had come to pay them back in the same *vein*[7].

Having *acceded*[8] defeat at the hands of the twins, Shatrughana went straight to his brother Rama. This time Lakshmana was sent with the army but he too had to return defeated.

Now was the turn of Rama to come with the huge army to free his *yagya* horse. The next morning Rama arrived from Ayodhya with his huge army. Rama took a look at the twins and he was totally *smitten*[9] by their charm. He called them and asked them their identity. His quiet and polite manner seemed to melt the boys a bit and finally they told him that their names were Luva and Kusha and their mother was the revered daughter of the great king Janaka of Mithila. They had been brought up by Sage Valmiki and that they had no information about the dynasty of their father whom they had never seen. Just then Rama saw Sage Valmiki come out of the ashram and fell to the feet of the great sage.

Valmiki blessed Rama.

As Rama got up to confirm about what the two boys had told him, his eyes fell on Sita who stood behind the sage, still as *radiantly*[10] beautiful as when he had first seen her in Mithila.

---

5. *envisaged – foreseen*
6. *haughtiness – arrogance*
7. *vein – streak*

8. *accede – assent*
9. *smitten – besotted*
10. *radiantly – vividly*

An Understanding

Q & A

Q. Who performed the *Ashwamedha Yagya*?

Ans. _____

_____

Q. Where was the horse stopped?

Ans. _____

_____

Q. Who defeated Shatrughan and his army?

Ans. _____

_____

Q. Why did Rama feel smitten by the charms of the boys?

Ans. _____

_____

Q. Whom did Rama see standing behind Sage Valmiki?

Ans. _____

_____

Common Error & Correction

Rewrite these sentences after placing punctuation marks and capital letters at the right places

1. as rama got up to confirm about what the two boys had told him, his eyes fell on sita who stood behind the sage still as radiantly beautiful as when he had first seen her in mithila

   _____

2. having acceded defeat at the hands of the twins shatrughana went straight to his brother rama

   _____

3. what a lovely horse let us catch it we shall take it to the ashram and keep it as a pet said luva and kusha

   _____

4. no holy sacrifice especially *yagya* can be successful without the presence of husband and wife together

_____

_____

5. pride always has a fall sooner or later ravana too paid for his pride.

_____

_____

Food for Thought

In your own words and perception, describe the feelings of Rama and Sita as they come to face each other after separation of so many years.

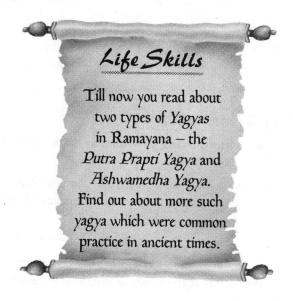

Life Skills

Till now you read about two types of *Yagyas* in Ramayana – the *Putra Prapti Yagya* and *Ashwamedha Yagya*. Find out about more such yagya which were common practice in ancient times.

30

Sita Embraces Mother Earth

"Sita, Sita," Rama whispered moving forward to touch her. Then suddenly he stopped as if he remembered something.

Luva and Kusha were surprised that Rama not only knew Sage Valmiki, he even knew the name of their mother.

Sita drew her two sons along with her and came forward, "My lord, these are your twin sons, Luva and Kusha. Forgive them if they have done any harm."

Rama's eyes filled with affection. These two brave boys had defeated his entire army but won his heart. They were his own sons. They had proved they were the true heirs of *Surya Vansha*.

Luva and Kusha looked at each other in surprise. Rama was their father! They had grown up hearing the stories of his great deeds...he was their father! Then why was their mother not living with him? Why were they living in an ashram and not in a palace with him?

These questions *whirled*[1] in their minds. When Valmiki asked Rama to take back his family to Ayodhya with him, Sita looked at Rama. Rama stood still, looking at Sita. But the moment Sita's eyes turned towards him, he looked away. Instead of enquiring about her well-being, he was trying to ignore her. There was a doubt *lurking*[2] in his mind. He did not have the courage to take her back to Ayodhya as his queen because there were still people of Ayodhya to be considered. He valued their opinion more than anything in this world. His duty as a king was far more important than his own desire as a husband.

Sita sensed the hesitation in his eyes. He still did not want to take her back. But he wanted his sons. And she very well knew her sons would never leave her. She saw the three most adorable men in her life, her husband and her two sons, standing together. Their glory lit up the forest. Their *valour*[3] shone in their heroic deeds. They looked so bright together. Ayodhya was where her sons belonged, not in this ashram. She felt that she was coming in their way. This happy picture was complete even without her.

Sita's eyes *glinted*[4] with tears threatening to come out in *spurts*[5]. She had devoted her whole life in the prayer of her husband. She always supported and respected him. She had admired him for being a king whose sole duty was to live and act for the happiness of his people even at the cost of his personal happiness.

But this was not justice. How could such a loyal king be unjust towards his own wife just to please his subjects? But who was she to question his judgment. She knew she had lost it all. She could not control her tears now.

With tears flowing down her cheeks, Sita folded her hands and bowed her head, "Mother Earth, if I have been pure and dutiful towards my husband all my life; if I have done any good deeds in all my life; if my heart is pure and my love for Rama true, then take me in your lap. I do not wish to take even a single breath in this place."

There was silence all around as everyone watched *mesmerised*[6].

Sita, bowed to everyone, stood there with her hands folded, and eyes closed,

---

1. *whirled – twirled*
2. *lurking – creeping*
3. *valour – courage*

4. *glinted – sparkled*
5. *spurt – gush*
6. *mesmerised – enthralled*

waiting for Mother Earth to *engulf*[7] her and free her from this life of pain and misery.

There was a loud clap of thunder and the earth slowly *split*[8] apart at Sita's feet. The tiny *cleft*[9] soon grew into a deep hollow. There arose a golden throne borne on the heads by powerful serpents. On the throne, sat the goddess of the earth. The sight may have terrified others but it brought a sense of relief to Sita. She looked at Rama and her two sons for the last time. There was a look of pride in her eyes. Time and again she had proved her purity and chastity to Rama who always failed to recognise her. It was the final goodbye to a life full of pain and false *accusations*[10].

Mother Earth took Sita in her lap and sat her beside her on her throne. There was a shower of divine flowers which covered Sita as the throne disappeared inside the earth and the ground closed over them as if it had never opened up.

Luva and Kusha watched their mother disappear in horror. They began to cry bitterly and loudly. They were overcome with grief. Since birth, the only family they had known was their mother. And today, she was gone so suddenly.

Rama was shocked at the turn of events. Rama fell down on earth *pleading*[11] the Goddess of Earth to open up and return his Sita back to him. He promised to stay with her till the end of his life. He cried to give up the kingdom and live a life of hermit with Sita by his side. But he was too late.

---

7. *engulf – swallow up*
8. *split – crack*
9. *cleft – fissure*

10. *accusations – allegations*
11. *pleading – beseeching*

An Understanding

Q & A

Q. What did Valmiki ask Rama to do?

Ans. _____

_____

Q. Who sensed hesitation in Rama's eyes?

Ans. _____

_____

Q. Who were the three most adorable men in Sita's life?

Ans. _____

_____

Q. Whom did Sita summon to take her away?

Ans. _____

_____

Q. Why did Rama plead to the Goddess of Earth?

Ans. _____

_____

Make Sentence

Write antonyms for these words and make sentences with them

1. backward

_____

_____

2. answer

_____

_____

3. king

_____

_____

4. wife

_____

_____

5. daughter

_____

_____

6. wrong

_____

_____

7. sad

_____

_____

8. hatred

_____

_____

9. injustice

_____

_____

10. appear

_____

_____

11. laugh

_____

_____

12. close

_____

_____

13. death

_____

_____

14. early

_____

_____

15. appear

_____

_____

Food for Thought

Why did Rama not enquire about Sita's well-being and turn his face away when she looked at him? Was it guilt, hatred, or shame? Write a small paragraph describing Rama's feelings in your own words and perception.

Life Skills

We have seen many incidents of earth opening up in the form of earthquakes. Did Sita enter the earth during an earthquake or was it a pure divine event — we would never know. But we can find out more about earthquakes, tsunamis, and other natural calamities.

31

Rama's Sons

For a long time, Rama *gazed*[1] at the place where Sita had disappeared, then he put his arms around Luva and Kusha.

"Your mother was a great soul. Now we must return to Ayodhya as per her wishes. Come with me, my sons," Rama told them.

Luva and Kusha looked at Sage Valmiki who nodded towards them, "Yes, children, go with your father. This is what your mother wanted. She knew she was coming in your way to return to Ayodhya, so she gave up her life. Your true place is in Ayodhya. In the ashram, you have learnt everything you could as my *disciple*[2]. Now it is time you learn to be princes. May God bless you." Valmiki placed his hand over their head as the two boys bowed down to touch his feet.

Lord Rama accompanied by his sons, proceeded towards Ayodhya. The whole of Ayodhya was decorated like a bride in the same way as it welcomed Rama when he had returned after fourteen years of exile with Sita.

A great procession marched through the streets of Ayodhya.

The boys were welcomed by their grandmothers and aunts at the palace. Soon they became familiar with everyone. There was happiness all around. Everyone was rejoicing on having found their heir.

With Sita gone, Rama had lost the *zeal*[3] to live. He felt tired and soon he decided to call it a day.

After bidding goodbye to all his near and dear ones, Rama requested the priests, councilors, and citizens to crown Bharata as the king to the throne of Ayodhya. But Bharata refused. Even other brothers refused. All the brothers were adamant on following Rama wherever he went. They did not intend to sit on the throne.

"Then come with me, if this is what you wish," Rama said after he placed Kusha on the throne of Ayodhya.

Turning towards Hanuman, Rama said, "You must stay on the earth forever

---

1. *gazed – looked*
2. *disciple – student*

3. *zeal – enthusiasm*

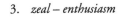

for the sake of your devotion to me. You must look after the people on earth in my absence."

Though Hanuman was sad that Rama was going to heaven leaving him forever, he felt happy at the *task*[4] assigned to him.

Followed by all the citizens of Ayodhya, Lord Rama and his brothers moved towards the banks of river Sarayu and entered the river to proceed towards heaven.

Rama's sons Luva and Kusha looked after his kingdom well. They grew up to be brave warriors and gentle, kind, and just rulers.

Today Rama exists in each and every particle of this universe. No force, no deluge can destroy his presence from this universe. Whenever there is trouble in any part of the world Rama's *glory*[5] manages it beautifully.

---

4. *task – duty*   5. *glory – magnificence*

An Understanding

Q & A

Q. What did Rama tell his sons after Sita disappeared in the earth?

Ans. _____

_____

Q. Whose permission did Luva and Kusha seek before going with Rama?

Ans. _____

_____

Q. Where did Rama take Luva and Kusha?

Ans. _____

_____

Q. Why did Rama lose the zeal to live?

Ans. _____

_____

Q. Who sat on the throne of Ayodhya after Rama left for his final abode?

Ans. _____

_____

Comprehension

Read the following passage and answer the questions that follow.

Brahma was very happy with the karma performed by Rama on the earth. As a special gift to Rama he offered him a boon, "You've done a marvelous job on earth. I, therefore, allow you to enter heaven in any form you wish to choose."

Thus Rama decided to take Lord Vishnu's form and entered the river Sarayu with his brothers following him. The water closed on their heads. Soon the heavens opened and the celestials rained flowers on all of them.

Brahma spoke, "O gracious Vishnu, you are indestructible, immutable, glorious, and eternal. Give up maya and resume your Vishwa-Swaroopa."

Suddenly out of the waters arose the incredibly beautiful handsome form of Lord Vishnu laced with the discus, conch, mace, and lotus in his hands. Everyone bowed before him.

1. What made Brahma happy?

   _____

   _____

2. What boon did Brahma offer to Rama?

   _____

   _____

3. Which form was taken by Rama before entering the river Sarayu?

   _____

   _____

4. Who followed Rama into the water?

   _____

   _____

5. What did Brahma ask Vishnu to do?

   _____

   _____

6. Write any four adjectives Brahma used for Lord Vishnu.

   _____

   _____

7. What happened when Lord Vishnu gave up *maya* and showed his Vishwa-Swaroopa?

   _____

   _____

Food for Thought

Why did Rama coronate Kusha as king and not
Luva? Justify.

Life Skills

Ramayana sets many standards in relationships. When Rama decides to give up his throne, none of the brothers want to take it up and decide to follow him instead. This kind of devotion and selfless conduct seems to be a thing of past. Write a short story based on moral values which once formed a part of human life.

Morals in the Ramayana

*T*he Ramayana depicts the human code of conduct in clear words through Rama. The Ramayana also reinforces the need for thinking about the consequences before making promises, for if you make them you must keep them, no matter how hard it may be.

In the Ramayana Rama is not portrayed as a supernatural being, but as a human with all the shortcomings, who encounters moral dilemmas but who overcomes these by simply adhering to the *dharma* – the righteous way of living.

There are several instances narrated in the Ramayana which cast shadows on the pristine character of Rama and reinforce the theme of Rama struggling with mortal flaws and prejudices whilst struggling to follow the path of *dharma*. When Rama killed Bali to help Sugriva regain his throne, it was not in fair combat because Rama killed him while hiding behind a tree. When Sita was freed from Ravana's prison, Rama forced Sita to undergo an ordeal to prove her purity and later as the king, Rama abandoned her in her delicate state of health. All these show the weakness of his character.

Dharma-Artha-Kama-Moksha in the Ramayana

The concepts of *Dharma, Artha, Kama,* and *Moksha* are very old Hindu concepts. They are known as *Purusharthas*.

Dharma here means the duties and welfare one does for the society. Making wells, for example, is part of the *dharma* of a king.

Artha means earnings. The king has to see that there is enough income from taxes, the salaries of the employees are given at proper time, and the tax should not be more than 1/6 th or 16.6 % of a person's income.

Kama means pleasure. One is allowed to have pleasure but without affecting his duties and earnings.

Quiz Books
(प्रश्नोत्तरी की पुस्तकें)

02307 P • ₹ 110 • 144 pp   02304 P • ₹ 200 • 256 pp   02308 P • ₹ 120 • 128 pp   02310 P • ₹ 120 • 184 pp   02309 P • ₹ 96 • 104 pp   02303 P • ₹ 96 • 192 pp   02302 F • ₹ 120 • 256 p

Also available in Hindi ₹ 120

STUDENT DEVELOPMENT (छात्र विकास)

00503 P • ₹ 110 • 142 pp   10501 P • ₹ 96 • 152 pp   5645 D • ₹ 150 • 133 pp   02311 P • ₹ 96 • 112 pp   9076 D • ₹ 80 • 144 pp   10502 P • ₹ 96 • 144 p

COMPUTERS (कम्प्यूटर्स)   QUOTES/SAYINGS (उद्धरण/सूक्तियाँ)

02402 P • ₹ 100 • 104 pp   12401 P • ₹ 120 • 164 pp   00801 P • ₹ 96 • 132 pp   10803 P • ₹ 96 • 144 pp   00804 P • ₹ 125 • 187 pp

ENGLISH IMPROVEMENT (अंग्रेजी सुधार)

Learn sophisticate style of correct Englis writing! Polish you communication line and skill by usin effective and attractiv words modern reader and writers prefer Suitable examples fo easy applicatio provided.

03902 P • ₹ 120 • 64 pp   10802 P • ₹ 80 • 132 pp   03901 P • ₹ 88 • 230 pp   9437 A • ₹ 120 • 148 pp

POPULAR SCIENCE (लोकप्रिय विज्ञान)

9436 D • ₹ 110
136 pp (Bangla)

BESTSELLER

22121 P • ₹ 110/
136 pp (Tamil)

12101 S • ₹ 160/
136 pp

A how-to-do guide illustrating 81 innovative and contemporary science projects from physics, chemistry, biology and electronics, backed by an audio-visual CD. Indispensable for project presentations & science exhibitions.

02101 P • ₹ 160 • 120 pp

02103 P • ₹ 96 • 120 pp

12103 P • ₹ 96 • 120 pp

02201 P • ₹ 80 • 144 pp

02139 P • ₹ 110 • 160 pp

12140 P • ₹ 110 • 160 pp

02102 P • Rs. 495/- (HB) • 520 pp

BIOGRAPHIES (आत्म कथाएँ)

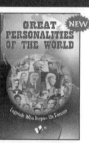

03704 P • ₹ 150 • 264 pp

03701 P • ₹ 135 • 228 pp

13703 P • ₹ 96 • 152 pp

03705 P • ₹ 120 • 176 pp

03702 P • ₹ 80 • 120 pp

CHILDREN SCIENCE LIBRARY (चिल्ड्रंस साइंस लाइब्रेरी)

Set Code: 02122 S

Set Code: 12138 S

All books available at WWW.vspublishers.com